EVERYDAY

Chineasy™

EVERYDAY
The World of Chinese Characters

BY SHAOLAN 曉嵐
with illustrations by NOMA BAR

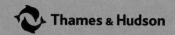
Thames & Hudson

First published in the United Kingdom in 2016 by
Thames & Hudson Ltd, 181A High Holborn, London WC1V 7QX

Chineasy Everyday: The World of Chinese Characters © 2016 Chineasy Ltd
(chineasy.com)

Art Director: ShaoLan Hsueh 薛曉嵐
Author and Concept: ShaoLan Hsueh 薛曉嵐
Illustrator: Noma Bar

British Library Cataloguing-in-Publication Data
A catalogue record for this book is available from the British Library

ISBN 978-0-500-29226-6

Manufactured in China by Imago

To find out about all our publications, please visit
www.thamesandhudson.com.
There you can subscribe to our e-newsletter, browse or
download our current catalogue, and buy any titles that are in print.

CONTENTS

The Calligrapher's Daughter

ShaoLan and her children,
MuLan and MuAn, painted in 2011
by Judith Greenbury, the artist
and friend who inspired ShaoLan
to turn Chineasy into a book

I grew up in a little town outside Taipei called Yingge (鶯歌), which is famous for the production of porcelain and for its many artist studios. My maternal grandfather, known as A-Gong (阿公), was a renowned professor of ceramic art. My father, a young mathematician and mechanical engineer, decided to become one of A-Gong's students after he married my mother. Years later, he also became a professor of ceramic art and a master in glazing.

Our house was piled high with pieces of art – both finished and unfinished – created by my ceramicist father and calligrapher mother.

My sisters and I grew up surrounded by clay, ink and paint. I loved playing with my father's potter's wheels and my mother's brushes. My parents, however, hoped that I would not pursue an artistic career. They wanted me to study finance, accounting or law, so as to gain a well-paid job, known as 金飯碗 (a 'golden rice bowl'). I defied their wishes and studied science. They probably began to despair as they saw me hanging around with computer nerds and putting all the royalties I earned from writing books on software into an internet venture. By that time, in 1995, I was studying for an MBA, but I was channelling all my energies into building this internet startup. It was a wonder that I even graduated.

By the late 1990s the internet company I co-founded had turned into one of the major players in Asia. It was an exciting time, and my work frequently took me around the world. As I travelled the globe, many people teased me the moment they saw my reading material – a very thick Chinese dictionary. It looked like a brick. I shrugged and continued diving into those beautiful characters and fascinating stories and etymology. The years spent watching my mother practise her calligraphy might have planted the seeds in my head, and my nerdy mind started seeing patterns whenever I stared at the characters.

I left Taipei in early 2001 and eventually moved to the UK. I had to get to grips with an entirely different culture, so I stored away the Chinese books I had brought with me and spoke my first language only with family and friends back in Taiwan. As my children, MuLan and MuAn, were growing up, I struggled to encourage them to learn Chinese. They simply found it too hard. I could not find anything to help their studies, so I took on the task myself. It was the beginning of our fascinating journey. They saw my Chineasy TED Talk and thought it was cool. My children became my art directors, helping me with the look of each drawing, and they remain my most critical judges.

The family project, the result of our collective creative endeavour, came to be appreciated by many others. As I became consumed by a heavy workload and constant travel, my children protested and told me they didn't like Chineasy any more; they asked me why I was working so hard, as they thought Chineasy was supposed to be private. I tried to explain how we could help others by making Chineasy publicly available. They did not want to listen, and turned their attention to gaming and mobile app coding. My children remind me of the young rebel I once was. Yet, years later, here I am, building on the wealth of knowledge that my own parents gave me.

One day, once they have found their own paths, I hope my children will be proud of Chineasy, and understand why I'm doing it. Let our family motto be: I create, therefore I am!

HOW TO USE THIS BOOK

What's new?

The first Chineasy book, *Chineasy: The New Way to Read Chinese*, demonstrated how it is possible to gain a knowledge of Chinese characters in a short space of time by focusing on the 'building blocks' of the language. *Chineasy Everyday* continues to use this building-block principle (see opposite), but don't worry: you don't need to have read the first book in order to understand and enjoy this new book. The two books are complementary but independent. *Chineasy Everyday* will help you to learn even more Chinese characters, and also discover more about Chinese culture and everyday life in China.

The Chinese language reflects the history, culture and philosophy of the country and its people. With the help of the illustrations in this book, you will learn many new characters; but *Chineasy Everyday* will also teach you the stories behind these characters, as well as fascinating Chinese myths.

The book is structured by topic to help you navigate and find the phrases most suited to your interests and situation. Each chapter is devoted to a theme (for example, people, animals or travel), and contains relevant, easy-to-learn characters, phrases and sentences – along with insights into Chinese life.

At the end of each chapter there is a section called 'Let's explore further', which contains interesting stories relevant to the chapter theme or tips for learning more about the Chinese language. The additional characters on p. 150, at the end of Chapter 7, represent just a small selection of the number of characters you can build based on what you've learned in the previous chapters. In fact, by the time you reach the end of the book, you will have learned over 400 of the most common and useful Chinese characters – that's an impressive amount of knowledge!

The index, starting on p. 242, lists every character and phrase taught in *Chineasy Everyday*, and provides you with its traditional and simplified forms (see p. 18) and its pinyin (see p. 19).

Chineasy methodology

Throughout the book, we use three important Chineasy terms: 'building block', 'compound' and 'phrase'. Let me explain what these mean.

Building block
The Chinese language is traditionally taught through a series of between roughly 180 and 215 radicals. These radicals form the characters we use to read, write and speak Chinese. When I say 'building block', I'm referring to some of the most common and simple radicals that we use to build many characters and phrases. An example is the character 木, which means 'tree' or 'wooden' (see p. 49).

Compound
One building block (e.g. 'tree' 木 or the character 火 for 'fire'; see p. 47), or an alternate compound form of the building block (e.g. ⺣ 'fire'), can be combined with one or more other characters to make a compound character: one 'fire' on top of another is 'burning hot' 炎; if we double up 'tree', we get 'woods' 林. Compound characters can also comprise two or more different building blocks; see the examples on the next page.

Phrase
Both 'building block' and 'compound' refer to single-character words in Chinese. If we place two or more independent characters next to one another, we get a phrase (e.g. two 'burning hots' next to each other are 'blazing' 炎炎). In Chineasy methodology, a phrase may translate as either a single word in English (as in 'blazing') or a group of words.

building block – tree   compound – woods   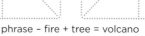
phrase – fire + tree = volcano

In compounds, a whole new character is created; in phrases, the placement of characters next to one another gives a new meaning to the collection of characters. This principle of building blocks is what makes Chineasy so easy!

Character composition

When you are learning to read Chinese, it's helpful to understand something about the structure, or composition, of the characters. If you can recognize the composition, it should enable you to remember the characters more easily. These are the five different structures you will encounter most frequently.

1. Single
The characters that are structured in this way are usually the most ancient in the Chinese language, and are generally pictographs – that is, pictures of the objects that they represent. Characters with this structure cannot be divided into smaller components.
Examples: 'sun'/'day' 日, 'moon'/'month' 月, 'fire' 火, 'water' 水

2. Left-right
As the language of our ancestors became more sophisticated, single-body characters were combined to create a variety of structures. One such structure is left-right.
Examples: 'bright'/'tomorrow' 明, 'woods' 林, 'good'/'OK' 好

Occasionally you will see a three-part character (left–centre–right), such as 'lion' 獅 or 'monkey' 猴.

3. Top-bottom
Another way in which to combine single-body characters is the top-bottom structure.
Examples: 'man'/'male' 男, 'star'/'planet' 星, 'dad' 爸

When three building blocks are stacked on top of one another, we form a top-centre-bottom structure, such as 'grass' 草 or 'tea' 茶.

4. Triplet
'Triplet' refers to a character that can be roughly divided into three components. It could be one on the top and two on the bottom, such as 'crowd' 众, 'flame' 焱 or 'forest' 森, or two on the top and one on the bottom, such as 'to sit' 坐.

5. Surround
There are several subdivisions of this structure, including fully surrounded and partially surrounded, which means that the character has an opening on the top, bottom, right or left.
Examples: 'to return' 回, 'rain' 雨, 'bed' 床

Reading 101

Is Chinese read horizontally or vertically? Chinese can be read in either direction. In fact, you can read from left to right, right to left, or top to bottom. The only direction you won't find is bottom to top.

Today the most common style is from left to right, in the same way that English, French, Spanish or German are read.

In some ancient literature or on road signs in China, you will sometimes see phrases written from right to left. This can prove to be odd when you have literature that mixes both English and Chinese. I once saw a book cover that had the English title running from left to right and the Chinese title running from right to left!

If you are trying to read vertically (for example, you quite often have to do this if you are reading scrolls), then you would read from right to left, starting with the first vertical line on the right from top to bottom, and then moving towards the left edge of the scroll.

| big | eat | big | drink |

make a pig of oneself

The 'Six Writings'

There are different kinds of Chinese characters, based on their derivation and formation. Over the centuries, scholars have held differing views on how characters should be categorized, but the best-known method of classification is called the 'Six Writings' 六書/六书 (liu[4] shu[1]; see p. 19 for an explanation of pinyins), developed during the Han dynasty (206 BCE –CE 220). Some knowledge of these principles will help to consolidate your learning – but don't worry about trying to remember it all!

1. Pictographic 象形 (xiang[4] xing[2])

A pictograph depicts an object such as an animal, a plant or a tool. The ancient Chinese drew their family members (man, woman, child, even dog), their surroundings (tree, grass, stone, water and mountain) and their means of making a living (cow, sheep, chicken, knife and boat). Some 600 or so pictographic characters were created in this way thousands of years ago. Over the centuries, however, many of these characters have changed either slightly or significantly. You can see many of them used as building blocks in this book. The beauty of Chineasy is that, by knowing only relatively few characters, you can combine them to create many more characters.

2. Indicative 指事 (zhi[3] shi[4])

Abstract concepts cannot be expressed easily by a drawing. Characters that indicate a concept – known as indicative characters or simple ideograms – are created in two ways: either by adding a stroke to an existing pictographic character (by drawing a plank beneath 'tree' 木, we create 本, which means 'foundation' or 'origin'), or by using symbols to indicate a new concept (examples include 'up'/'above' 上 and 'down'/'below' 下, which are adaptions of the character for 'one', 一. In this instance, 一 represents the earth, and the additional components indicate things being 'above' or 'below' the earth).

3. Compound ideogram 會意/会意 (hui[4] yi[4])

Compound ideograms, created by putting two or more building blocks together, are characters that represent more complicated concepts, abstract ideas or even objects. When the 'sun' 日 and the 'moon' 月 shine together, they make the character 明, meaning 'bright' or 'brightness', because the sun and the moon were once the major sources of light. 明 also means 'tomorrow' – after a day and a night. Two other examples: the source of 'power' 力 on a 'farm' 田 was 'man' 男; start a 'fire' 火 in the 'woods' 林, it starts 'burning' 焚. In Chineasy, there are many examples of characters formed in this way; it's a simple means of increasing your Chinese vocabulary.

4. Phono-semantic 形聲/形声 (xing² sheng¹)

The majority of Chinese characters belong in this category, which is sometimes also known as pictophonetic. As civilization progressed, our Chinese ancestors required characters and phrases to represent more subtle and sophisticated meanings. Instead of creating more individual symbols from scratch, they combined two or more building blocks to make phono-semantic characters; these have a pictographic component indicating the meaning, and another component indicating the sound of the whole character. Most modern characters were created in this way. For example, 'mum' 媽 (ma¹) is a combination of 'woman' 女 (nü³) and 'horse' 馬 (ma³); 女 indicates the meaning, while 馬 provides the pronunciation. The character 'to drink' 喝 (he¹) is a combination of 'mouth' 口 (kou³), providing the meaning, and 曷 'a shouting noise' (he²), indicating the pronunciation.

5. Mutually explanatory 轉注/转注 (zhuan³ zhu⁴)

Characters of this type share a similar meaning or sometimes a similar pronunciation, and therefore they can be used to 'explain' one another. For example, the characters 老 (lao³) and 考 (kao³) share the same semantic radical, 耂, so they are mutually explanatory: 老 means 'old' (see p. 125) and although 考 nowadays usually means 'to test' or 'to verify', it was used in ancient literature to mean 'long life' or 'aged'.

6. Phonetic loan 假借 (jia³ jie⁴)

A phonetic loan is a character that was created to mean one thing but has been 'borrowed' to represent something else on the basis of it having the same pronunciation. For example, the character 來 (lai²) was originally a pictograph of 'wheat', but the character was 'borrowed' to express 'to come'. Over the years another character for 'wheat', 麥 (mai⁴), was created, so 來 came to mean 'to come' alone. Another example is the character for 'north': 北 (bai³) originally meant 'back (of the body)'. Later on, however, 背 (bai⁴) was created to mean 'back' by combining 北 and the compound form of 'flesh', 月 (see p. 212), leaving the sole meaning of 北 as 'north'.

Although you'll see references to pictographs and phono-semantic (or pictophonetic) characters in this book, Chineasy methodology does not place great emphasis on the 'Six Writings'. Rather, Chineasy aims to use the most intuitive and effective method to allow non-native learners of Chinese to master basic characters in a way that is both systematic and enjoyable!

The development of writing styles

Chinese characters have evolved throughout history owing to changes of political regime, geographic expansion and the need to address social progress. There are five major historical Chinese writing styles: 'oracle-bone script' 甲骨文 (*c.* 1400 BCE), 'bronze script' 金文 (*c.* 1600–700 BCE), 'seal script' 篆書 (*c.* 220 BCE), 'clerical script' 隸書 (*c.* 200 BCE) and 'regular script' 楷書 (often called 'standard script'; *c.* 200 BCE). You will see references to most of these styles in this book. Each writing style has its own distinct features. Oracle-bone script is a set of characters etched on to animal bones or pieces of turtle shell that were then used for divination. Despite its pictorial nature, it developed into a fully functional and mature writing system. Bronze script (金 means 'gold' or 'metal'; see p. 50) refers literally to 'text on metals', as these inscriptions were largely found on ritual bronzes such as bells and cauldrons. The development of seal script witnessed the removal of curved or lengthy strokes; Chinese characters written in this style became roughly square in shape. By the time of the introduction of regular script, strokes had become smoother and straighter, and thus the characters were clearer and much easier to read and write.

In modern Chinese, regular script is most commonly used in writing and printing, while the earlier writing styles are used as calligraphic art forms. My calligrapher mother can write poems in seal script, clerical script, regular script and even cursive script (草書). Following the invention of the movable-type process, Song and Ming type styles came into use, just as Arial, Times New Roman and Helvetica are popular typefaces today for alphabetical languages. Nowadays our computers offer dozens of typeface choices.

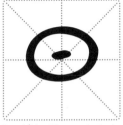

'sun'/'day' in oracle bone

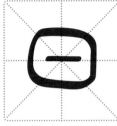

'sun'/'day' in seal script

'sun'/'day' in clerical script

'sun'/'day' in regular script

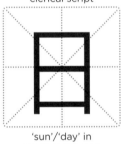

'sun'/'day' in modern Chinese

Writing 101

Chinese characters usually comprise two or more strokes. When you are writing, it's important to draw these strokes in the correct order. A particular method of writing characters was developed in CE 300, and since that time every Chinese child has learned how to write using the so-called Eight Principles of Yong (永字八法). There are eight common strokes you see in written Chinese. The character 永 (yong³) shown at right, which means 'forever', is often used to demonstrate these strokes.

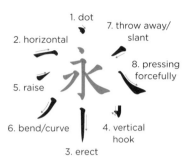

1. dot
2. horizontal
5. raise
6. bend/curve
3. erect
4. vertical hook
7. throw away/slant
8. pressing forcefully

1. 點/点 (dian³; dot) Place a dot at the top of the character for 'king' 王 to make 'master' 主. Add a dot on the right, between the two bottom strokes of 'king', to make the character for 'jade' 玉.

2. 橫 (heng²; horizontal) Draw this stroke from left to right. If a character has more than two horizontal strokes, always draw the top one first.

3. 豎 (shu⁴; erect) A vertical line drawn from top to bottom.

4. 豎鈎 (shu⁴ gou¹; vertical hook) This stroke looks the same as 豎 except for the tiny hook at the bottom.

5. 提 (ti²; raise) A flick up and to the right.

6. 彎/弯 (wan¹; bend/curve) A tapering curve, usually down to the left, and drawn quickly.

7. 撇 (pie³; throw away/slant) A short, downwards stroke, always drawn from right to left.

8. 捺 (na⁴; pressing forcefully) Start at the top and move to the bottom right. You can lift your pen a bit towards the end.

When you write Chinese characters, you also need to pay attention to the length of each stroke. At first glance, the two characters on the right look alike, but look carefully and note how the lower horizontal stroke is longer in 'soil'/'earth' 土 (tu³), while the upper horizontal stroke is longer in 'scholar' 士 (shi⁴).

soil/earth

Everyone who studies Chinese has to practise on grid paper when they first learn how to write. Each character has to be drawn neatly inside a square. See how, on p. 11, a single 'tree' fits into a square the same size as the square used for 'two trees'. In order to fit two trees side by side in the square, you must draw thinner trees. A character, whether it's a building block (such as 'tree' 木) or a compound (such as 'woods' 林), fits within one square. A phrase, on the other hand, is spaced across two or more squares – see, for example, 'volcano' 火山 on p. 11.

scholar

Traditional or simplified?

Written records of the Chinese language, in oracle-bone script, have been discovered dating as far back as the 14th to 11th centuries BCE, during the Shang dynasty. Since that time, the use of Chinese characters has spread to neighbouring countries, including Japan. Japanese kanji share an incredible number of characters (about 2,000–3,000) with Chinese; sometimes there is a slight variation in meaning, but usually the meaning is either identical or differs only slightly.

lightning/electricity
(traditional Chinese)

Over the past few thousand years, Chinese dialects have evolved at different rates depending on where they are spoken. In comparison, written Chinese has changed relatively little. However, from 1949, in an attempt to promote mass literacy, the Communist Party on mainland China began simplifying traditional Chinese characters. This process involved removing or altering the number of strokes in traditional characters, making them easier to read and write.

lightning/electricity
(simplified Chinese)

Traditional and simplified forms of Chinese still share a great number of characters, and in real life – just as in the case of British English and American English – you will come across both forms. English speakers are familiar with not only different spellings ('colour' vs 'color') but also the use of different words to refer to the same thing ('flat' vs 'apartment', 'rubbish' vs 'garbage').

Many educational institutions teach only traditional Chinese (which is the written language of Taiwan and Hong Kong) during the first term of study, as it provides the foundation for learning the language. Simplified Chinese might look easier, but in fact many beginners find traditional Chinese more straightforward. This is because traditional forms of characters often resemble more closely the shape of the objects that they represent. For example, you can still see the four legs of a 'traditional horse' (馬; see p. 105), but a 'simplified horse' (马) has lost its legs. In some cases, however, the simplified form of a character is much easier for a beginner. Take, for instance, the character for 'crowd' (see p. 63): the simplified form is 众 (three people together – easy!); the traditional form is 眾.

Chineasy teaches both traditional and simplified forms. For ease of learning, the traditional form of a character is indicated first. We specify in the character captions the rarer cases where the simplified form is used instead of the traditional one (e.g. 'dot'/'o'clock' on p. 26). Where no distinction between forms is noted, the traditional and simplified forms of the character are the same.

Speaking 101

Mandarin is the most widely used Chinese dialect. It counts over 960 million native speakers out of a total of over 1.2 billion Chinese speakers. To teach Mandarin Chinese to non-native speakers, most teachers use pinyin, the standard phonetic system for transcribing the sound of Chinese characters in the romanized alphabet.

Chinese is a tonal language, so the pinyin system uses a series of either numerals or glyphs to represent tone. For instance, the pinyin for 'person' can be written as either ren[2] or rén. Chineasy uses the numerical pinyin system.

After every English translation, you will see a word in parentheses followed by a number; this acts as a guide to the pronunciation of the character. For example, 人 person (ren[2]).

Tone 1	Tone 2	Tone 3	Tone 4	No number
high level tone	rising tone	falling rising tone	falling tone	neutral tone

Even though there are several different spoken Chinese dialects, they all share the same written characters; it is only the pronunciation of these characters that differs from one dialect to another.

Most Chinese characters have just one pronunciation in Mandarin, but there are some exceptions. For example, when the character 長 (simplified form: 长; see p. 132) is used as an adjective, meaning 'long', it's pronounced as 'chang[2]'; when it is used as a verb, meaning 'to grow', it's pronounced as 'zhang[3]'.

Note also the character 不, meaning 'no' or 'not' (see p. 122). It is usually pronounced as 'bu[4]'. However, it becomes 'bu[2]' when it is followed by a fourth-tone character, for the simple reason that a second tone followed by a fourth tone sounds better than two fourth-tone characters together. Similarly, 一, the character for 'one' (see p. 22), is normally pronounced as 'yi[1]', but it becomes 'yi[2]' when it is followed by a fourth-tone character, and 'yi[4]' when it is followed by a first-, second- or third-tone character.

CHAPTER 1

....

NUMBERS, TIME & DATES

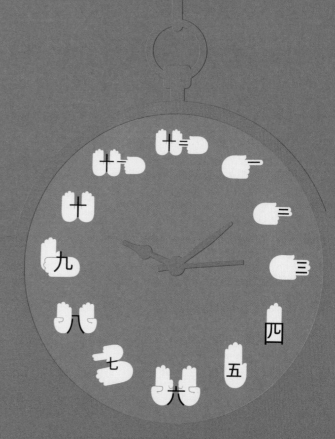

Numbers 1 to 10

一 one (yi¹)

The character for 'one' is a simple horizontal line. It comprises a single stroke, known as the *heng* stroke, and, fittingly, is the first character a Chinese child learns to write. When this character is used in a phrase, its pronunciation varies; see p. 19.

二 two (er⁴)

The character for 'two' is as easy as the number one! We just add a slightly longer horizontal line below 一 (one). The number two is considered auspicious in Chinese culture. There is a Chinese saying: 'Good things come in pairs.'

三 three (san¹)

The character for 'three' continues the simple pattern of 'one' and 'two' by adding a third stroke, thus 三. 'Three' often indicates 'many'. In Confucianism and Taoism (see p. 83), three represents Heaven, Earth and mankind.

四 four (si⁴)

The number four is considered unlucky because it sounds very similar to 'death' 死 (si³). This explains why some high-rise buildings omit all floor numbers that include 'four', such as 4, 14, 24 and 40–49. A waiter in a restaurant says 'a table for three plus one' (三加一; san¹ jia¹ yi¹), rather than 'a table for four'.

五 five (wu³)

This number is associated with the five elements (see the next chapter) and the Emperor of China. This is why there are five archways at Tiananmen Gate, which was reconstructed in 1651.

六 six (liu⁴)

Originally, this character was a pictograph of a hut, but now 六 is used exclusively to mean 'six' – a lucky number in China, especially in business. The very common idiom 六六大顺 (liu⁴ liu⁴ da⁴ shun⁴) means 'double six'. People use it to express best wishes at New Year or at weddings or on birthdays, or good luck when playing the lottery.

七 seven (qi[1])

Seven symbolizes 'togetherness', and is auspicious for relationships. In traditional Chinese religions, 49 (7 x 7) is the number of days a deceased person's spirit will remain among the living. The funeral ceremony therefore traditionally lasts over 49 days, when prayers are said every seven days for seven weeks.

八 eight (ba[1])

In the Mandarin and Cantonese dialects, the number eight sounds very similar to 'prosperity' and 'fortune' respectively, which makes it a very lucky number throughout the Chinese-speaking world. For example, the 2008 Summer Olympics in Beijing began at 8 p.m. on 8 August 2008. That's 8 p.m. on 8/8/2008! How lucky!

Counting from 11 to 99

Learning to build more numbers in Chinese is easy if you know the numbers 1 to 10 and the following three rules.

For the numbers 11 to 19, we use the number 十 (ten) plus whichever number follows it. For example:

11 = 10 (十) + 1 (一) = 十一
12 = 10 (十) + 2 (二) = 十二
And so on; therefore, 19 is 十九.

The character for 'zero' in Chinese is 零 (ling[2]). However, it is very common to see people using the Arabic numeral 0 or a circle, O, especially when talking about numbers or dates.

For the numbers 20, 30, 40 ... to 90, it's also quite straightforward to count numbers by 10s:

20 = 2 (二) x 10 (十) = 二十
30 = 3 (三) x 10 (十) = 三十
90 = 9 (九) x 10 (十) = 九十

The other numbers up to 99 require some simple mathematics. For example:

22 = 2 (二) x 10 (十) + 2 (二) = 二十二
45 = 4 (四) x 10 (十) + 5 (五) = 四十五
99 = 9 (九) x 10 (十) + 9 (九) = 九十九

There you have it: now you can count from 1 to 99 in Chinese! See p. 36 to continue with higher numbers.

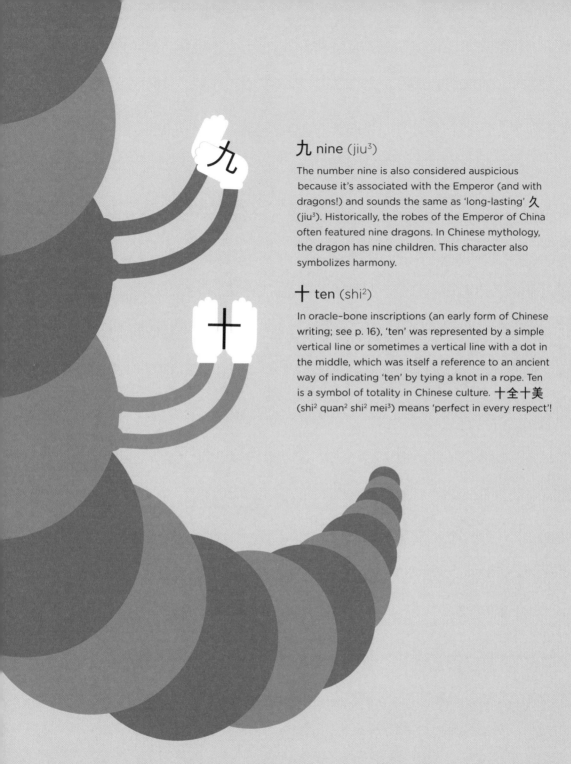

九 nine (jiu³)

The number nine is also considered auspicious because it's associated with the Emperor (and with dragons!) and sounds the same as 'long-lasting' 久 (jiu³). Historically, the robes of the Emperor of China often featured nine dragons. In Chinese mythology, the dragon has nine children. This character also symbolizes harmony.

十 ten (shi²)

In oracle-bone inscriptions (an early form of Chinese writing; see p. 16), 'ten' was represented by a simple vertical line or sometimes a vertical line with a dot in the middle, which was itself a reference to an ancient way of indicating 'ten' by tying a knot in a rope. Ten is a symbol of totality in Chinese culture. 十全十美 (shi² quan² shi² mei³) means 'perfect in every respect'!

Telling the time

点 dot/o'clock
(dian[3])

点 is a really useful
character to know.
It also means 'point',
'aspect', 'drop', 'spot'
or 'place'. In the context
of telling time, it is used
as 'o'clock', meaning an
exact hour. This is the
simplified form of the
character; the traditional
form is 點.

一点 one o'clock
(yi[1] dian[3])

If we add 'one' in front of 'o'clock', it means 'one o'clock'. Telling the time is so simple!

One o'clock = 'one' 一 + 'o'clock' 点 = 一点 (or 一點 in its traditional form)

八点 eight o'clock
(ba[1] dian[3])

We follow the same pattern for 'eight o'clock'.

Eight o'clock = 'eight' 八 + 'o'clock' 点 = 八点 (or 八點 in its traditional form)

See p. 131 to learn 'half past' the hour.

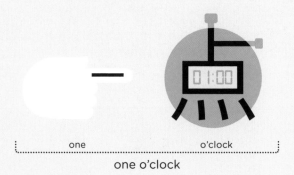

one | o'clock

one o'clock

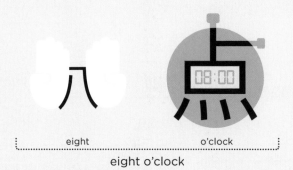

eight | o'clock

eight o'clock

年 year (nian[2])

The earliest form of this character, in oracle-bone inscriptions, depicted a man carrying his harvest home. Gradually, its meaning evolved to become 'year'. I like to remember it by thinking that, without the aid of modern agricultural technologies, our ancestors would have been able to harvest their crops only once a year.

月 moon/month (yue[4])

The traditional Chinese calendar is based on the lunar cycle, so in addition to meaning 'moon', the character 月 also means 'month'. The dates of many Asian holidays and festivals are still determined by the traditional calendar.

日 sun/day (ri[4])

Originally, the character for 日 was a circle with a dot in the middle, so it looked more like a 'sun' than the modern character. Eventually, the dot in the centre became the horizontal line we see in the middle today, and the circle became a rectangle. This character also means 'day', because we think that the day starts when the sun comes up and finishes when the sun goes down.

明 bright/
tomorrow (ming²)

When the sun (日)
and the moon (月)
are shining together,
they create a character
meaning 'bright' or
'brightness'.

This character can also
mean 'tomorrow' or
'immediately following in
time'. I like to imagine it
by thinking that when the
sun and the moon have
both completed their
journey through the sky,
one day is gone — so it's
tomorrow!

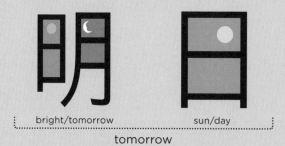

bright/tomorrow   sun/day

tomorrow

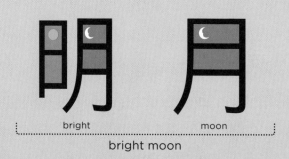

bright   moon

bright moon

bright/tomorrow   year

next year

明日 tomorrow
(ming² ri⁴)

bright/'immediately following in time' + day = next day/tomorrow

Although the character 明 can mean 'tomorrow', you more frequently see the phrase 明日, where 明 is used as an adjective to describe the noun 日 'day'. We can also use this phrase to refer to an unspecified date in the near future.

There is nothing wrong in saying that 明日 also means 'bright sun', but people tend not to use it this way.

明月 bright moon
(ming² yue⁴)

bright + moon = bright moon

When we combine 'bright' 明 and 'moon' 月, we get 'bright moon'. This phrase is often used as an adjective that means 'bright', 'clear', 'explicit' or 'wise'. You could argue it's not wrong thinking that 明月 means 'next month'. However, the conventional expression for 'next month' is 下個月 (xia⁴ ge⁴ yue⁴).

明年 next year
(ming² nian²)

bright/'immediately following in time' + year = next year

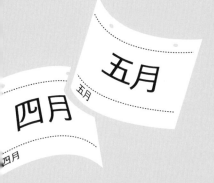

The calendar

The traditional Chinese calendar is lunar (based on the moon), which is very different from the Gregorian calendar, which is commonly used in Western countries. However, almost everyone today, including the Chinese, uses the Gregorian calendar for official business. So when you learn the names of the months and the date in Chinese, they all translate literally – easy!

THE MONTHS

When stating the months in Chinese, you just need to add the character 月 (moon) after the relevant number between 1 and 12. In the traditional calendar, months are measured by the phases of the moon. One lunar cycle is one month. Even though we are talking about Gregorian months here, you can still remember each month as 'one moon cycle', 'two moon cycles', etc. Here are a few examples of the months in Chinese:

January = 'one' 一 + 'moon' 月 = 一月
[literally] 'one moon cycle'

February = 'two' 二 + 'moon' 月 = 二月
[literally] 'two moon cycles'

December = 'twelve' 十二 + 'moon' 月 = 十二月
[literally] 'twelve moon cycles'

DAYS OF THE MONTH

The days of the month are written in a similar way to the months of the year: you just need to add the character 日 (sun/day) after the relevant number between 1 and 31.

So, the days of the month in Chinese are as follows:

1st day of the month = 'one' 一 + 'day' 日 = 一日

2nd day of the month = 'two' 二 + 'day' 日 = 二日

31st day of the month = 'thirty-one' 三十一 + 'day' 日 = 三十一日

THE DATE

In English, we may say either 'January 7th' or '7th January', but in Chinese the word order for phrases related to time always goes from 'big' to 'small'. This means, we start with the year, then move to the month, then the day, then finally the time.

For example, 7 January is 一月七日 ('one' 一 + 'moon' 月 for 'January', then 'seven' 七 + 'day' 日).

And 31 December is 十二月三十一日 ('twelve' 十二 + 'moon' 月 for 'December', then 'thirty-one' 三十一 + 'day' 日).

Qixi Festival: Chinese Valentine's Day
7th day of the 7th month in the Chinese calendar

Qixi (七夕; qi¹ xi¹) is a traditional festival celebrating the annual meeting of separated lovers in Chinese mythology. It's also called 'Double Seventh' because it always falls on the 7th day of the 7th month (七月七日; qi¹ yue⁴ qi¹ ri⁴) of the traditional lunar calendar.

The myth concerns the love story between Cowherd and Weaver Girl (牛郎與織女/牛郎与织女; niu² lang² yu³ zhi¹ nü³). Although there are many versions of the story, the earliest-known reference is dated more than 2,600 years ago.

This is the version I learned when I was young. A long time ago, there lived a poor Cowherd. His parents had died, and he lived with his cruel and mean brother and sister-in-law. A farmer took pity, and offered him a daily meal and a bed of straw in a cowshed. In return, Cowherd looked after the farmer's old ox.

One night, guided by the Ox, Cowherd spotted seven beautiful fairies bathing by moonlight in a river. Dazzled by the gorgeous sight, Cowherd grabbed one of the fairies' robes hanging on the branches of a tree. Seeing this stranger approaching, six of the fairies rushed to recover their robes and flew away, leaving their youngest sister in the river. This fairy was Weaver Girl, the fairy of the Vega star. Cowherd promised to return her robe on condition that she married him. Weaver Girl decided to stay on Earth, abandoning her job as the Vega fairy. The couple married and had two children. Cowherd worked in the field, while Weaver Girl taught humans how to grow silk and to weave.

The Heavenly Mother was furious when she learned about Weaver Girl's behaviour. She descended from Heaven and forced Weaver Girl to return to the sky, leaving devastated Cowherd and their young children behind. The Ox told Cowherd that he could use his skin after his death. It turned out that the Ox was the constellation Taurus. He returned to the sky, leaving his body to Cowherd. Using the skin as a cape and taking his children with him, Cowherd headed to Heaven to look for Weaver Girl.

As the family was about to reunite, the Heavenly Mother cast a spell to create the Milky Way, preventing the couple from getting close to each other. Cowherd became the Altair star, looking across the Milky Way towards his beloved Vega. Each year, on 7 July, a flock of magpies form a bridge across the sky to reunite the lovers for one day.

Dragon Boat Festival
5th day of the 5th month in the Chinese calendar

The Dragon Boat Festival (龍舟節/龙舟节; long² zhou¹ jie²), also known as the Duanwu Festival (端午節/端午节; duan¹ wu³ jie²), is a traditional festival widely celebrated in China, Taiwan, Hong Kong and overseas Chinese communities. It falls on the 5th day of the 5th month (五月五日; wu³ yue⁴ wu³ ri⁴) of the traditional lunar calendar. There are many different origin stories relating to the festival. The most common is that it started in reaction to the suicide of the famed poet and statesman Qu Yuan.

Qu Yuan lived during the Warring States Period (475–221 BCE), a time when seven kingdoms – Qi, Chu, Yan, Han, Zhao, Wei and Qin – vied for hegemony. Qu Yuan was a statesman of the Chu state and trusted by its king. Over time the Qin state succeeded in invading the other six states. In an attempt to save the Chu people, Qu Yuan advised the king to form an alliance with the Qi state, but corrupt courtiers turned the king against him. As a result, Qu Yuan's suggestion was ignored, and he was exiled. His wise counsel was no longer heard, and the Chu state eventually fell to the Qin state. In 278 BCE, on learning that the Chu had been defeated by the Qin, Qu Yuan, in great distress, took his life by drowning in the Miluo River, in what is now the northeastern part of Hunan Province. The legend goes that, on witnessing his suicide, the men on the shore rushed to the nearest boats they could find and raced out to save Qu Yuan, but they were too late. Later, to preserve his body, the villagers threw rice balls into the river to distract the fish from eating the flesh, and beat drums and hit the water with paddles to scare away evil spirits. These rice balls became known as *zongzi* (粽子; zong⁴ zi), and are traditionally served during the festival.

Although the origin of the Dragon Boat Festival is tragic, the modern festival is one of celebration. The three most common festival activities are the eating of *zongzi*, the drinking of realgar wine (realgar is a toxic substance traditionally used as mosquito repellent) and, of course, dragon boat racing. Families today go down to the river to watch strong young men compete against one other in an attempt to win luck for their villages.

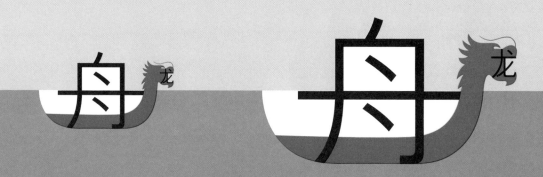

百 hundred (bai³)

This character looks like 'one' (一) on top of 'white' 白 (bai²). The earliest form of the character depicted an ancient container with a horizontal symbol at its top to indicate the amount of material inside. It has come to mean 'hundred'.

百 is often used in phrases to refer to 'many'. For example, 百草 ('100 grass'; bai³ cao³) means 'herb collection' (see p. 204 for 'grass'); 百货 ('100 goods'; bai³ huo⁴) means 'general merchandise'; 百姓 ('100 surnames'; bai³ xing⁴) means 'common people'.

千 thousand (qian¹)

The ancient usage of this character is very different from its modern usage; it used to indicate a man walking endlessly. Its modern meaning is 'thousand'. I like to imagine that the man must be walking for a thousand miles to get to his destination. 千 can also mean the precise number 1,000.

As in the case of 百, 千 is often used to describe 'many'. For emphasis, 千 and 百 are used together as a phrase (千百; qian¹ bai³) to mean 'a lot'.

元 dollar (yuan²)

In oracle-bone inscriptions, this character depicted a man kneeling down. The two horizontal lines at the top (二) represent the man's head, while the bottom part (儿) represents kneeling. The initial meaning of the character was 'head' or the 'beginning' of something, since the head was emphasized in the original script. Today it has been extended to mean 'dollar'.

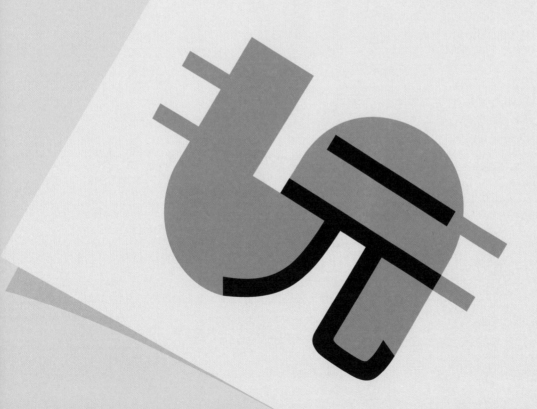

生 birth/life
(sheng¹)

The original form of this character depicted a handful of sprouts emerging from the earth. The idea of shooting sprouts was extended to the current meaning: 'birth', 'life', 'to be born', 'to give birth', 'to grow' or 'to generate'.

When 生 is used as an adjective, it means 'raw' or 'fresh'.

Chinese philosophy on birth & life

Chinese society is heavily influenced by Buddhism, Taoism and Confucianism (see p. 83). These belief systems offer rather differing views on birth, life and death.

Confucius asked, 'If we don't know yet about life, how can we know about death?' (未知生, 焉知死?). He wanted people to seize the moment and focus on the present. In Buddhism, death is not the end of life; it is merely the end of the body we inhabit during this life. The concept of karma, or the law of cause and effect, dominates people's attitude to birth and life and their behaviour on a day-to-day basis. For Lao Tzu and Chuang Tzu, two ancient Taoist philosophers, life and death are just part of the natural cycle of the universe; therefore, there is nothing to fear.

Most Chinese people, however, tend to avoid the topic of death. Some people regard it as an unknown territory they do not wish to go near. A fear of this subject affects their daily life. For example, the number four is considered inauspicious because it sounds very similar to 'death' (see pp. 23 and 42), and giving someone a clock (see p. 43) or white or yellow flowers is regarded as taboo because they indicate death.

一生 one's life
(yi¹ sheng¹)

one + life = one's life

This phrase can also mean 'lifetime'.

生日 birthday
(sheng¹ ri⁴)

birth + day = birthday

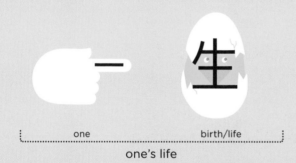

one   birth/life

one's life

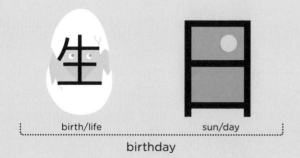

birth/life   sun/day

birthday

Let's explore further

Lucky & unlucky numbers in Chinese culture

Lucky numbers:

六 'six' (liu⁴) implies everything will go smoothly, because it sounds like 流 (liu²), meaning 'flowing', 'smooth' or 'frictionless'. 六 is considered especially lucky when it appears in multiples.

八 'eight' (ba¹) sounds like 'fortune' 發/发 (fa¹; see p. 143).

九 'nine' (jiu³) sounds the same as 'long-lasting' 久 (jiu³).

Unlucky numbers:

四 'four' (si⁴) sounds like 'death' 死 (si³).

十四 'fourteen' (shi² si⁴) sounds like 'ten die' 十死 (shi² si³).

1,000 vs. 1,0000: how to form large numbers

When we write large numbers over 999 in English, we insert a comma after every three digits from the end, to indicate separate groups of thousands. In Chinese, large numbers are based on tens of thousands (万 is 'ten thousand'), so imagine that the comma is moved one digit to the left, after every four digits from the end:

Every four digits	Chinese	English
1,0000 (4 zeros)	一万 (yi² wan⁴) one + ten thousand	ten thousand (10,000)
100,0000 (6 zeros)	一百万 (yi⁴ bai³ wan⁴) one + hundred + ten thousand	one million (1,000,000)
1,0000,0000 (8 zeros)	一億 (yi² yi⁴) or 一亿 (simplified) one + hundred million	one hundred million (100,000,000)

元旦 New Year's Day (yuan² dan⁴)

There are several Chinese expressions for 'New Year's Day'. One of them is 元旦. 元 means 'beginning' (see p. 37), and 旦 means 'sunrise' (see opposite). The meaning 'beginning of sunrise' is extended to refer to the start of the year – New Year's Day.

More compound characters

On p. 11, I talk about the term 'compound' in Chineasy methodology. An example of a compound character you have seen in this chapter is 明 'bright' (see p. 30). Here are a couple of other compound characters comprising building blocks you have learned in this chapter.

旦 sunrise (dan⁴)

日 'sun' + 一 'one' = 旦
Doesn't this character look like the sun rising above the line of the horizon?

早 early morning (zao³)

日 'sun' + 十 'ten' = 早
Doesn't this character look like the sun above a flagpole? And when do we usually hoist a flag? In the early morning!

Chinese gift-giving: clocks or no clocks?

Gift-giving is a very important part of Chinese culture and is associated with Confucianism and its concept of 'face', meaning 'honour'. Gift-giving began as a way of displaying filial piety and respect for one's elders. It has long been part of the Confucian mantra of maintaining harmony within one's family, friends and society at large through respect and ritual.

Traditionally, because the giving of gifts is symbolic of the esteem you have for the recipient, etiquette and superstition dictate the items that people give one another. For instance, it is considered unlucky to gift a clock of any type, because 送鐘/送钟 (song⁴ zhong¹; 'to give a clock as a present') sounds the same as 送終 (song⁴ zhong¹; 'funeral ritual'). However, it is interesting to note that, although clocks are deemed hugely unlucky, luxury watches are very popular gifts – so the times are changing!

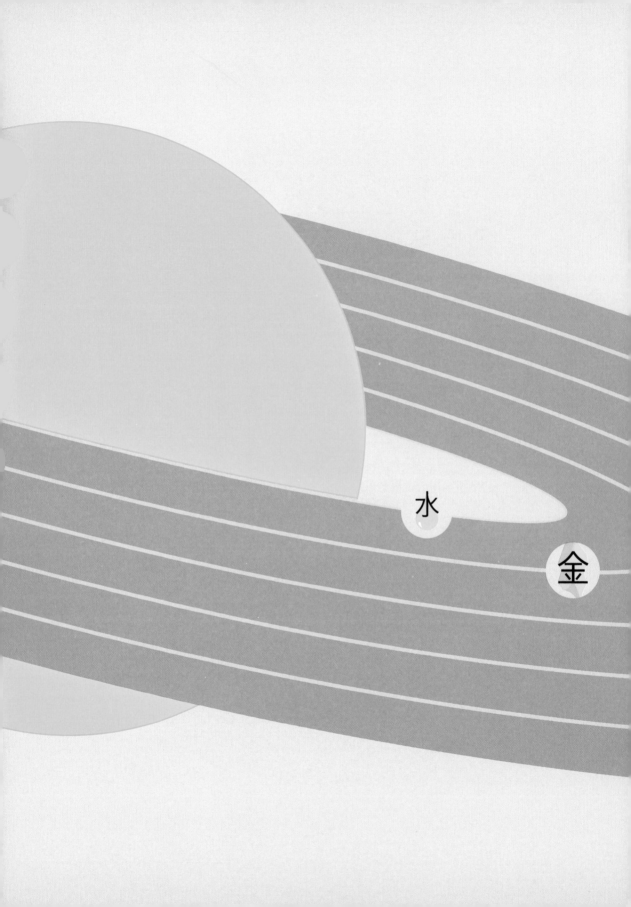

CHAPTER 2

THE SOLAR SYSTEM &
THE FIVE ELEMENTS

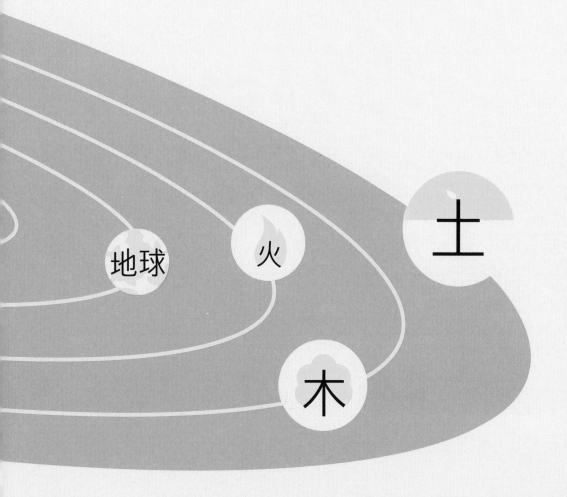

水 water (shui³)

This character originally had a winding line in the centre, showing how water flows, and dots on both sides, representing drops of water. Imagine it as one main river with smaller ones flowing into it on either side.

氵 is the form of the character used as a component in certain compounds. A shortened version of 水, 氵 is commonly known as 'three dots of water' (三点水; san¹ dian³ shui³).

淼 wide expanse of water (miao³)

When we triple 水 'water', we get 淼, meaning 'wide expanse of water', 'flood' or 'infinity'. This is a rather advanced character, so it's an excellent opportunity to show off to your Chinese-speaking friends!

火 fire (huo³)

This character depicts the shape of a flame. 'Fire' is a common theme in Chinese mythology, and there was a hierarchy of gods in charge of 火.

灬 is the form of the character used as a component in certain compounds, such as 'to cook' 煮 (zhu³) and 'to fry' 煎 (jian¹).

炎 burning hot (yan²)

Two fires together mean 'burning hot'. When this character is used in a medical context, it means 'inflammation'. This makes perfect sense, because the Latin root of 'inflammation' is *inflammare*, 'to set alight'.

焱 flames (yan⁴)

Repeat 火 three times and you have a roaring fire – flames. Watch out!

炎炎 blazing (yan² yan²)

burning hot + burning hot = blazing

土 soil/earth (tu³)

The earliest form of this character depicted a lump
of mud on the ground. The horizontal line at the
bottom (一) represents the ground, and the shape
of the lump evolved to become a cross (十). In
addition to 'soil', 土 can mean 'earth' or 'ground'.
When the character is used as an adjective, it
implies something unsophisticated.

木 tree/wooden (mu⁴)

In oracle-bone inscriptions, this character depicted a tree with roots in the earth and two branches reaching towards the sky. Over time, the branches became a single horizontal line (一) and the tree trunk was kept as a vertical line (|). The roots became similar to two arms falling down, one towards the left side and one towards the right.

When it is used as an adjective, 木 can mean 'wooden'. For example, 木床 (mu⁴ chuang²) is 'wooden bed' and 木門 (mu⁴ men²) is 'wooden door'. The character 樹/树 (shu⁴) is also commonly used to mean 'tree'.

林 woods (lin²)

When we double 木 'tree', we get 林 'woods'. The compound character 林 can also be used as a Chinese surname, spelled 'Lin' in English.

森 forest (sen¹)

When we triple 木 'tree', we get 森 'forest'. The phrase 森林 (sen¹ lin²) can also mean 'forest'.

金 gold/metal (jin¹)

The earliest form of this character depicted copper ore cast in a metal container, and meant 'metal'. The character has now been extended to mean 'gold' or 'money'.

鑫 symbolizing prosperity (xin¹)

What could be more prosperous than having a lot of gold (金) in business! 鑫 symbolizes 'prosperity'. You frequently see this compound character used in names of shops or even in people's first names.

The concept of Wu Xing

Some people call 水, 火, 土, 木 and 金 the Chinese 'five elements'. The word 'element' is misleading because, unlike the Western system of four elements, in Chinese culture these five may refer not only to natural matter. We call the theory of and dynamics between these five 'Wu Xing' 五行 (wu³ xing²); 五 is 'five', and 行 means 'movement'.

In many traditional Chinese fields of study, a system of five phases is used to describe interactions and interrelationships among phenomena. This doctrine of five phases has two cycles – a generating (生; sheng¹) cycle and a destruction/ control (克; ke⁴) cycle. In the generating cycle, wood feeds fire; fire creates earth (or ash); earth bears metal; metal enriches water (in the same way that water with added minerals is often considered more beneficial than plain water); and water nourishes wood.

In the destruction cycle, wood parts earth (in the way that roots push through the ground); earth absorbs, holds back or dirties water; water douses fire; fire melts metal; and metal chops wood.

The five phases are used to describe the seasons. Wood represents spring, as it's a period of growth, generating wood and creating vitality. Fire represents summer, because it's a period of flowering and swelling, bursting with fire and energy. Metal refers to autumn, a time of harvesting and collecting. Water indicates winter, a period of retreat, when all is still. Earth then represents four transitional seasons.

Wu Xing presumes that all phenomena in the universe can be broken down into five elemental qualities, and so this framework is used in Chinese philosophy, astronomy, military strategy, traditional medicine, nutrition and cooking theory, martial arts, astrology, Feng Shui (see p. 100) and musicology. In traditional Chinese medicine (see p. 151), for example, the liver and gallbladder are associated with wood, the heart and small intestine with fire, the stomach with earth, the lungs and skin with metal, and the kidneys and bladder with water. The five-phase theory is applied in both diagnosis and treatment.

In traditional Chinese music, since the time of the Zhou dynasty (c. 1046–256 BCE) there has been a belief that 'correct' music, which brings harmony to nature, involves instruments correlating to the five phases. Confucianism, one of the major Chinese philosophies, emphasizes that a correct form of music is important for the cultivation and refinement of the individual. Furthermore, formal music following the circle-of-fifths theory was considered to be both morally uplifting and the symbol of a good ruler and stable government.

星 star/planet
(xing[1])

The character for 'star' is a combination of 'sun' 日 and 'birth'/'to be born' 生. The ancient Chinese regarded the sun as a similar object to a star: one ruled the day, the other ruled the night. They were correct in their thinking; the sun was born at the centre of our solar system, but it is just one star among billions in the galaxy.

星 can refer not only to a star in the sky, but also to a star, or celebrity, in the entertainment industry.

This character can also mean 'planet', as a shortened form of the phrase 星球 (xing[1] qiu[2]). 球 means 'ball' (see p. 190).

....

明星 bright star/ celebrity
(ming[2] xing[1])

bright + star = bright star/celebrity

The literal meaning of 'bright' 明 and 'star' 星 refers to those people performing well in their professions. 大明星 (da[4] ming[2] xing[1]) is a 'big star'; 小明星 (xiao[3] ming[2] xing[1]) is a 'minor celebrity'. See p. 120 for 'big' and 'small'.

The planets

Although the ancient Chinese did not differentiate between stars and planets, they noticed that the movements of the five visible planets (see below) were different from those of other celestial bodies. They even understood that the planets orbit the sun. Instead of coining a separate character to represent these five planets, our ancestors called them 行星 ('moving stars'; xing[2] xing[1]). The names of individual planets were based on their colours, which were matched to the five elements. See p. 191 for 'Earth'.

水星 Mercury (shui[3] xing[1])

Mercury is the 'water star' 水星 on account of its blue hue when observed from Earth.

金星 Venus (jin[1] xing[1])

After the sun and the moon, Venus is the brightest object in the sky. It is as shiny as gold, so Venus is the 'gold star' 金星. Venus was first mentioned in 詩經 (*The Classic of Poetry*; shi[1] jing[1]), the most ancient collection of Chinese poetry, comprising 305 works dating from the 11th to the 7th century BCE.

火星 Mars (huo[3] xing[1])

Today we understand that the red colour of Mars is the result of a layer of rust on its surface. However, our ancestors believed that the planet was alight, so Mars is the 'fire star' 火星.

木星 Jupiter (mu[4] xing[1])

Jupiter is the largest planet in our solar system. Its surface is covered with thick red, yellow, white and brown clouds, and for this reason it is named the 'wooden star' 木星. As early as the 2nd millennium BCE, the ancient Chinese determined that Jupiter takes twelve years to orbit the sun.

土星 Saturn (tu[3] xing[1])

The planet Saturn is yellowish tan in hue on account of its gaseous composition. This colour looks like the 'soil' 土 has dried out. Thus, Saturn became the 'soil star' 土星.

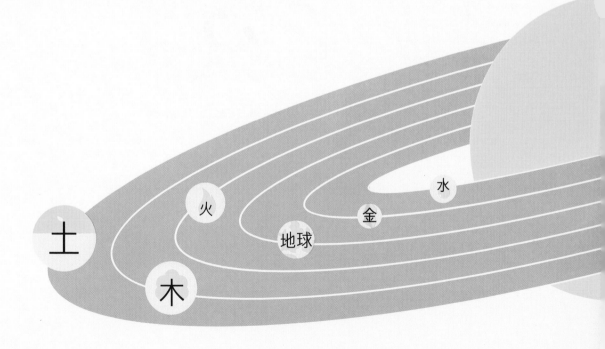

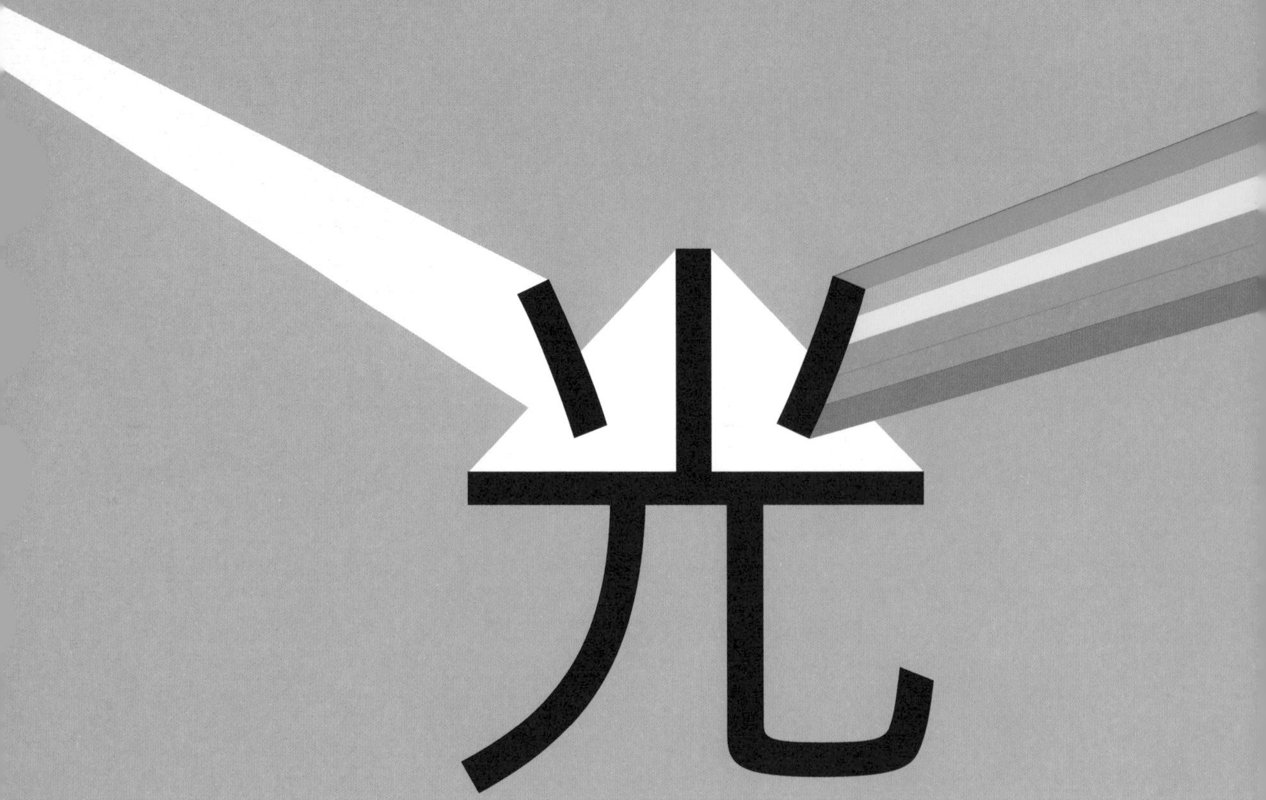

光 light (guang¹)

In ancient oracle-bone and bronze scripts, this character depicted a man kneeling down and carrying fire on top of his head. The meaning of the character has evolved to indicate 'light', which illuminates things and makes them possible to be seen.

光明 bright (guang¹ ming²)

light + bright = bright

The light (光) that is so bright (明) brings hope for the future, giving us something to look forward to. The phrase 光明 implies that the future is bright or promising.

光年 light year (guang¹ nian²)

light + year = light year

月光 moonlight (yue⁴ guang¹)

moon + light = moonlight

日光 sunlight (ri⁴ guang¹)

sun + light = sunlight

火光 firelight (huo³ guang¹)

fire + light = firelight

天 sky (tian¹)

In oracle-bone script, this character depicted a person with a head. In seal script, the head developed into a horizontal line, indicating the sky above one's head. So now this character is formed by 'one' 一 and 'big' 大 (see p. 63), showing a man opening his arms (大) and standing beneath the sky (一). It can also mean 'day' or 'heaven'.

天天 every day (tian¹ tian¹)

day + day = every day

Besides meaning 'every day' (as in 'each day'), this phrase can refer to the adjective 'everyday'.

明天 tomorrow (ming² tian¹)

bright/'immediately following in time' + day
= next day/tomorrow

This phrase can be used interchangeably with the phrase 明日 (see p. 31).

天生 innate (tian¹ sheng¹)

Here, 生 means 'to be born with'. 'Innate' refers to something that you've had since the day you were born. This phrase also means 'natural', as in an ability that you were born with.

陰 yin (yin[1])

Yin means 'feminine', 'female', 'cloudy', 'dark', 'shady', 'secret' or, in the context of electricity, 'negative'. The traditional form of this character, 陰, is a combination of 'hill' 阝 (fu[4]), 'cloud' 云 (see p. 89) and 'now' 今 (jin[1]). So, when clouds gather around the top of a hill, it is dark.

阴, the simplified form of the character, is a combination of 'hill' 阝 and 'moon' 月. One thing to note is that, as in the case of 'grass' 艹 (see p. 204), 阝 never exists as a stand-alone character.

....

光陰/光阴 time (guang[1] yin[1])

This phrase is a poetic way of describing a long period of time. It tends to refer to 'as time goes by'.

陽 yang (yang²)

陽, the traditional form of Yang, is a combination of 'hill' 阝, 'sun' 日 or 'sunrise' 旦, and 勿 (wu⁴). In the traditional form, 昜 means 'bright', having originally depicted 'sun' 日 with 'rays coming down' 勿. Some scholars believe that 勿 indicates the shape of the moon, and the combination of 'sun' and 'moon' means 'bright', because they were the primary source of light in the past.

阳, the simplified form of the character, is a combination of 'hill' 阝 and 'sun' 日. It means 'masculine', 'male', 'sun', 'solar', 'sunlight' or, in the context of electricity, 'positive'.

....

陽光/阳光
sunlight
(yang² guang¹)

阳光 is interchangeable with the phrase 日光 (see p. 54); both are very common.

太陽/太阳 sun
(tai⁴ yang²)

太 means 'extremely' or 'excessively' (see p. 63). 太阳 is interchangeable with 日 (see p. 28), although the former is used more frequently in conversation.

Let's explore further

The concept of Yin-yang

In Chinese philosophy, Yin and Yang are the fundamental 'building blocks' for comprehending how the universe works. In order to understand Chinese people and their culture, it is crucial to know something about the concept of Yin and Yang (Yin-yang).

Yin and Yang as a philosophical framework can explain all disciplines of knowledge in Chinese culture. Yin has slow, soft, pliable, diluted, cold, wet, cloudy, dark, shady, secret and passive qualities; it is aligned with water, earth, the moon, femininity, night-time and a negative electrical charge. Yang has fast, hard, solid, concentrated, hot, dry and aggressive qualities; it is aligned with fire, sky, the sun, masculinity, daytime and a positive electrical charge. Yin is withdrawn and inward-going, whereas Yang is outward-going and associated with growth. However, Yin and Yang are not static absolutes, and nothing is entirely Yin or completely Yang. In the same way that day gradually becomes night, the nature of Yin and Yang changes over time.

The 'Tai Ji' 太極/太极 (tai⁴ ji²; 'supreme ultimate') diagram shows that Yin (the largely pink area) and Yang (the largely blue area) are interdependent. They cannot exist without each other, and so must form a never-ending balancing act: as a state of utmost Yin is reached, Yang emerges. As one increases, the other decreases. Only together can they make a whole.

Any life form is a combination of Yin and Yang. In humans, man has his feminine side and woman her masculine side. In other parts of the natural world, the boundary between Yin and Yang may be even less distinct. Some flowers have both male and female parts, and some female fish have the ability to transform into male fish if the male population is too small.

In traditional Chinese medicine, one is healthy only when Yin and Yang are in balance. Without the warming properties of Yang, an excess of Yin may lead to poor circulation, cold limbs, pale skin and low energy. An excess of Yang, however, may result in headaches, nosebleeds, sore eyes and throat, a reddening of the skin, irritability and manic behaviour. Using the principle of Yin-yang, Chinese medicine is prescribed to compensate for any imbalance, with the aim of restoring a perfect equilibrium.

In philosophy, Yin and Yang represent truth and falsehood, meaning that nothing is absolutely true or totally false. For thousands of years, Chinese people have understood that there is no clear-cut boundary between yes and no, right and wrong, or good and evil.

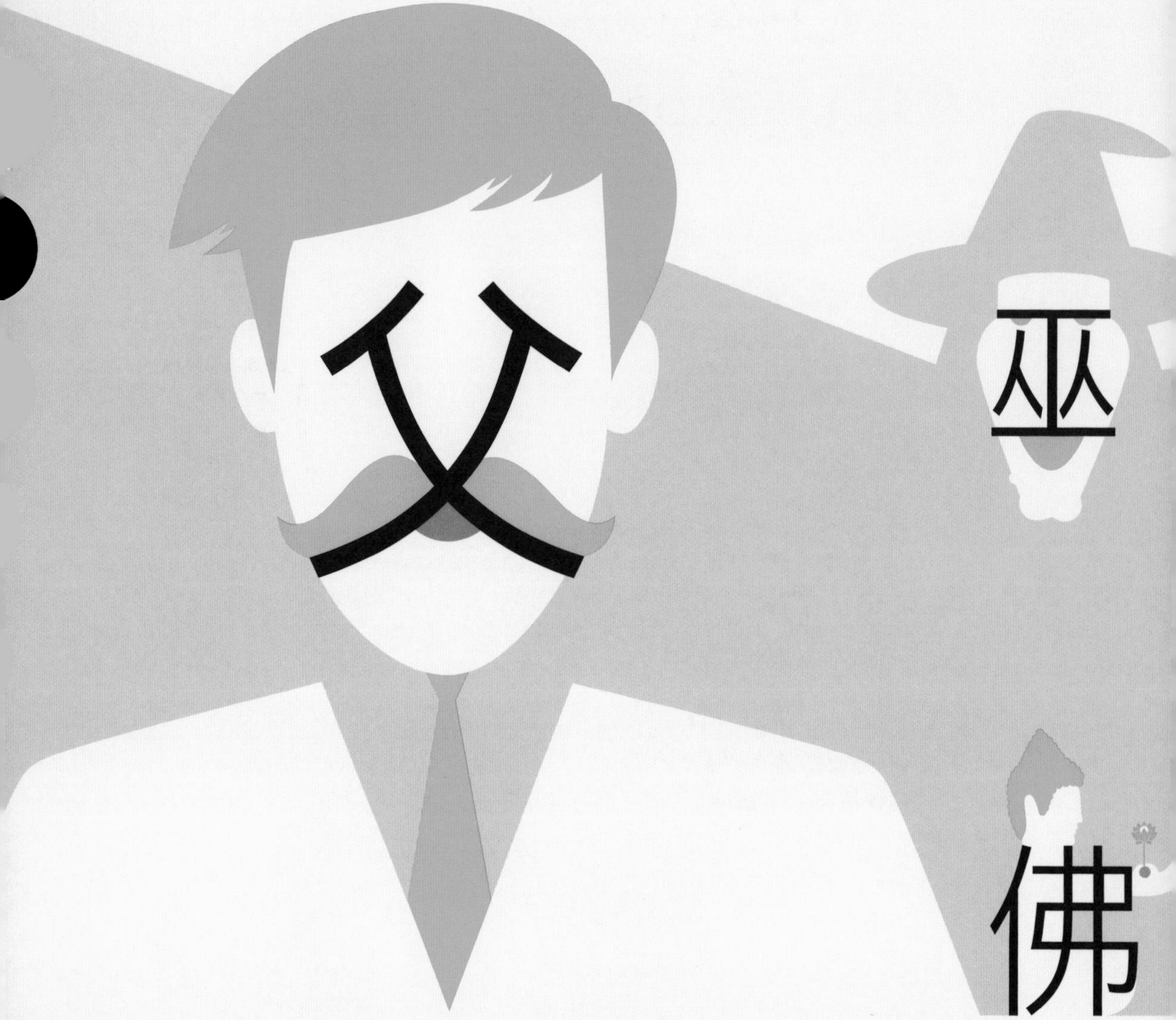
父
巫
佛

CHAPTER 3

PEOPLE

母

后

人 person (ren²)

The character for 'person' looks like the profile of a man walking. Most Chinese nouns make no distinction between singular and plural, so this character can also mean 'people'.

亻 is the form of the character used as a component in certain compounds. See 'Buddha' on p. 82 for an example.

从 to follow (cong²)

This character comprises two 'person' building blocks. One man leads, the other follows close behind. This is the simplified form of the character; the traditional form is 從.

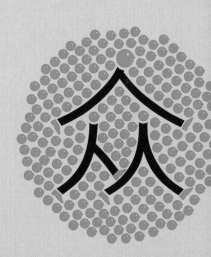

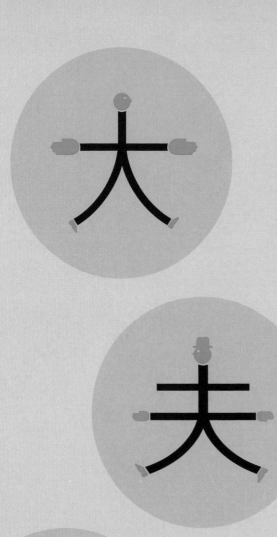

众 crowd (zhong⁴)

'Two's company, three's a crowd.' Three 'person' building blocks make a crowd. This is the simplified form of the character; the traditional form is 眾.

大 big (da⁴)

This character depicts a man stretching his arms wide. Imagine that he is saying, 'It was this big.' In addition to 'big' or 'large', 大 means 'the eldest' when used in reference to family members. For example, 哥 (ge¹) is 'elder brother', and 大哥 (da⁴ ge¹) is 'eldest brother'; 姐 (jie³) is 'elder sister', and 大姐 (da⁴ jie³) is 'eldest sister'.

夫 man (fu¹)

'Man' is the compound for 'big' with an extra line across the top of the character, like wide shoulders. This line represents the pins in a man's topknot hairstyle.

太 too much (tai⁴)

This compound comprises 'big' and a stroke under the character, suggesting something even bigger. It also means 'extremely' or 'excessively'.

人人 everyone
(ren² ren²)

person + person =
everyone

If we double up 'person',
we have 'everyone'.

大人 adult
(da⁴ ren²)

big + person = adult

The modern meaning of
'big-size person' is 'adult'.
Traditionally, this phrase
referred to people who
were of higher social or
official rank.

大众 public
(da⁴ zhong⁴)

big + crowd = public

A big crowd forms
the public.

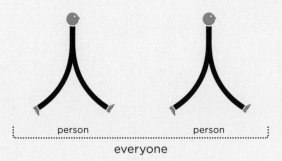

person   person

everyone

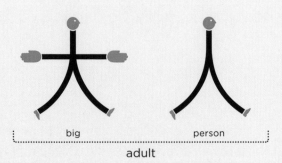

big   person

adult

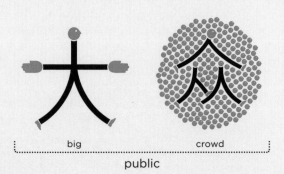

big   crowd

public

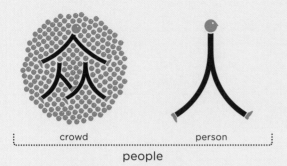

crowd   person

people

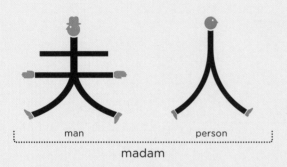

man   person

madam

too much/extremely   too much/extremely

Mrs/wife

众人 people
(zhong[4] ren[2])

crowd + person = people

A crowd is made up of many different people. This phrase also means 'everybody'.

夫人 madam
(fu[1] ren[2])

man + person = madam

In ancient China, a woman became her husband's property after marriage; she became her husband's person.

太太 Mrs/wife
(tai[4] tai)

extremely + extremely = Mrs/wife

This is very common usage. By doubling 'extremely', we get 'Mrs' or 'wife'. Ancient Chinese people flattered their boss by calling his wife 'extremely extremely'.

女 woman/female (nü³)

In oracle-bone inscriptions, this character depicted a
woman squatting down with her arms folded across
her body. This was a sign of submission, as women
were regarded as the possessions of men. I loathe
the origin of this character, so in Chineasy you see
it represented as an independent, witty and feminine
lady. She is her own person. In the context of family
relationships, 女 means 'daughter'. When used as an
adjective, it means 'female'.

女人 woman/female (nü³ ren²)

female + person = female person = woman/female

大女人 strong woman/feminist
(da⁴ nü³ ren²)

big + woman = strong woman/feminist

The phrase 大女人 means 'strong woman' or
'feminist'. When we refer to a woman with a
large figure, we use 胖女人 rather than 大女人.
胖 (pang⁴) means 'plump' or 'fat'.

男 man/male (nan²)

In oracle-bone inscriptions, this character depicted a man with 'power' or 'strength' 力 (see p. 195) in his arm, carrying out work in a 'field' 田 (tian²); the two components sat side by side. The character has evolved so that, in its modern form, 力 has relocated under 田 to become 男. When used as an adjective, this character means 'male'.

男人 man/male (nan² ren²)

male + person = male person = man/male

大男人 big man/chauvinist
(da⁴ nan² ren²)

big + man = [literally] big man = chauvinist

This phrase can be used literally to refer to a man who has a large figure, or it can be used figuratively as 'chauvinist'.

父 father (fu⁴)

This character depicts a hand holding an axe. In ancient China, the father was the person who used an axe to chop wood for the family, keeping them cosy and warm.

母 mother (mu³)

Since its earliest recorded form in oracle-bone inscriptions, this character has depicted a mother's breasts, in reference to feeding a baby. The original forms showed a woman on her knees or standing, but the modern form has shifted vertically and lost the long strokes that represented legs. I bet you'll remember 母 very easily now you know how it got its shape!

This character also means 'female' when referring to animals (see p. 117).

....

父母 father and mother/parents (fu⁴ mu³)

father + mother = parents

爸 dad (ba⁴)

A colloquial term,
this character is a
combination of 'father',
indicating the meaning,
and 'to hope' 巴
(ba¹), indicating the
pronunciation (see p. 15
for an explanation of
such phono-semantic,
or pictophonetic,
characters). When we
double up the character,
we get the phrase 爸爸
(ba⁴ ba), which means
'papa' and sounds
very similar to the
English word!

媽 mum (ma[1])

This character is a combination of 'woman' and 'horse' 馬 (see p. 105). It sounds like the English word 'mum'. When we double up the character, we get the phrase 媽媽 (ma[1] ma), which means 'mama' and also sounds very similar to the English word. The simplified form of the character is 妈.

....

爸媽 dad and mum (ba[4] ma[1])

The phrase is 'dad and mum', not 'mum and dad'.

子 son (zi^3)

This character may look at first glance like an uninspired doodle, but actually it's based on a rather cute oracle-bone inscription depicting a baby, complete with an oversized head and a few wispy hairs.

In addition to 'son', 子 can also mean 'child', 'seed' or 'small thing' (see 'electron', p. 98), and is sometimes used to refer to a young animal or young person, as in 'young fellow'.

You will also see 子 used as a suffix with other single-syllable nouns (the pronunciation is a little different in these cases). An example is 'car' 車子 (che^1 zi; see p. 154).

When we combine 'woman' and 'son', we form the very useful character 好, meaning 'good' or 'OK'; see p. 123.

father · son

father and son

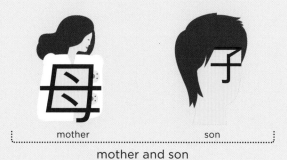

mother · son

mother and son

father · woman/daughter

father and daughter

mother · woman/daughter

mother and daughter

父子 father and son (fu⁴ zi³)

father + son

母子 mother and son (mu³ zi³)

mother + son

父女 father and daughter (fu⁴ nü³)

father + woman/daughter

母女 mother and daughter (mu³ nü³)

mother + woman/daughter

王 king (wang²)

The earliest form of this
character in oracle-bone
and bronze inscriptions
depicted a battleaxe,
a powerful weapon
in ancient times. In
those days, a ruler –
usually also the military
commander – would
use an axe to strike fear
into the hearts of his
enemies and urge his
soldiers forward. Thus,
this weapon became a
symbol of power, and
eventually came to
represent the highest
ruler in the land –
the king.

The character 王 is
also used as a Chinese
surname. The same
surname may be
spelled differently
('Wang', 'Wong' or 'Ong'),
depending on where the
family is from.

主 master (zhu³)

In oracle-bone inscriptions, this character depicted a torch above a pile of timber. In seal script, the character took on a more complex form, depicting (from top to bottom) the flame of the torch, the cresset (the metal bowl that holds the fuel and the flame), the torch pole and the torch holder. Today the character can mean 'host', 'owner' or 'god', but the most common definition is 'master'.

工 work (gong¹)

This character looks like an I-beam (a steel beam used in construction), which is a useful way to remember its meaning: 'work'. It was originally based on a primitive carpenter's square, used to measure right angles. The character hasn't changed much throughout its thousand-year history, and today is used in phrases that are work-related or refer to things requiring effort.

工人 worker (gong¹ ren²)

work + person = worker

人工 artificial (ren² gong¹)

person + work = [literally] person's work = man-made = artificial

女工 female worker (nü³ gong¹)

woman + work = [literally] woman's work or needlework = female worker

This phrase is interchangeable with 女工人.

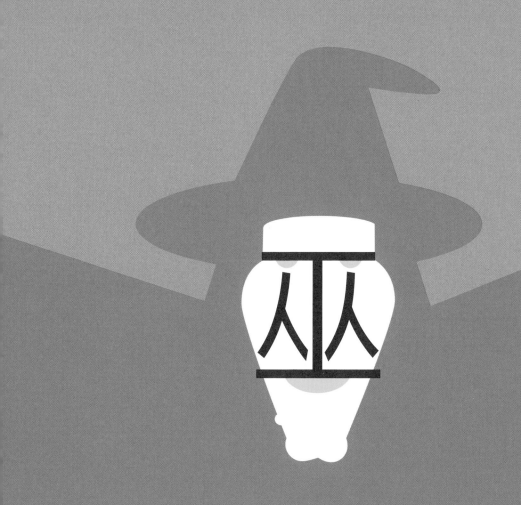

巫 shaman/witch (wu[1])

This character combines two 'people' building blocks with the character for 'work'. Can you imagine living at a time when 'witch' was a common job title? In ancient China, shamans were rather respected by emperors, officials and ordinary citizens alike for their role as spirit mediums, practising healing, prayer, sacrifice, divination and rainmaking.

This character isn't gender-specific, so sometimes you'll see it used to mean 'wizard'.

男巫 wizard (nan[2] wu[1])

male + witch/wizard = wizard

女巫 witch (nü[3] wu[1])

female + witch/wizard = witch

丑 clown (chou³)

In Chinese opera, the comic role is called 丑. The role is comparable to that of the fool in Shakespeare, but can be played by a man or woman, whether young or old. Clowns appeared in opera as early as the Spring and Autumn Period (771–476 BCE), and enjoyed the highest rank in the theatre.

During the simplification process that began in 1949 (see p. 18), the meaning of 丑 was extended to indicate 'ugly'. The traditional form of 'ugly' is 醜 (chou³), a combination of 'wine vessel' 酉 (see p. 205) and 'ghost' 鬼 (gui³).

± scholar (shi⁴)

By placing 'ten' + on top of 'one' —, we make the character for 'scholar'. In ancient China it was rare to be literate. Scholars were those who understood maths and literature. They were ranked as the highest level in the hierarchy of traditional Chinese society, followed by farmers, labourers and merchants.

天主 God
(tian¹ zhu³)

heaven + owner = the owner of heaven = God (particularly refers to the Christian God)

By adding 'religion' 教 (jiao⁴) to the end of this phrase, we form the phrase for 'Catholicism': 天主教 (tian¹ zhu³ jiao⁴).

天子 emperor
(tian¹ zi³)

heaven + son = the son of heaven (an imperial title of Chinese monarchs founded on the ancient philosophical concept the Mandate of Heaven) = emperor

女王 queen
(nü³ wang²)

female + king = queen

王子 prince
(wang² zi³)

king + son = king's son = prince

sky/heaven · master/owner

God

sky/heaven · son

emperor

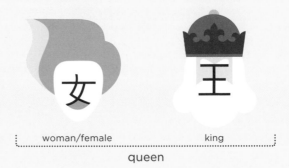

woman/female · king

queen

king · son

prince

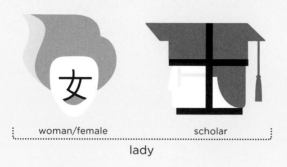

woman/female   scholar

lady

女士 lady
(nü³ shi⁴)

Scholars were highly respected in ancient China. To express courtesy, 'female scholar' means 'lady'.

主人 host
(zhu³ ren²)

This phrase has a few possible translations, depending on the context in which it is used. These include:

host + person = host (a person who hosts a party)

master + person = master (a person who has people working for him/her)

owner + person = owner (a person who owns something)

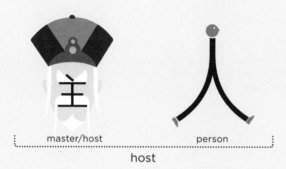

master/host   person

host

女主人 hostess
(nü³ zhu³ ren²)

female + master/host + person = hostess

男主人 host/owner
(nan² zhu³ ren²)

male + master/host + person = host/owner

woman/female   master/host   person

hostess

man/male   master/host   person

host/owner

佛 Buddha (fo²)

This character is a combination of the compound form of 'person' 亻 and 'not' 弗 (fu²). The composition of the character expresses well one of the basic concepts of Buddhism: it is not about the person (亻), it's a way of life and gives purpose to life. When we do 'not' (弗) have to consider a person's desires, we will be able to achieve enlightenment, and we will become the 'awakened one' – like Buddha.

Buddhism, Taoism and Confucianism – the pillars of Chinese society

Many Chinese people find that their lives are governed tightly by Buddhism, Taoism and Confucianism, even if they are not religious or they belong to a different faith. Together, these three doctrines provide guidance on how society should function and what its virtues should be.

Developed by Confucius (551–479 BCE), Confucianism is an ethical and philosophical system that guides people's behaviour in society. It came to prominence after Emperor Wu of the Han dynasty (206 BCE–220 CE) adopted it as the state ideology. The principles of Confucianism played a crucial role in the formation of the values, culture and mentality of the Chinese people. Confucianism also provided a strict social hierarchy – a convenient tool for those in power. In Confucianism, everyone fits within various types of social classification and rank. A person's place in this hierarchy governs both their behaviour and how they are judged by the community.

I grew up in a society where we were told that teachers and parents were always right. 天下無不是的父母 ('No parents could be wrong') was one of the idioms that every child could recite. We were told to be obedient. We learned how to behave within social guidelines in order to achieve harmony as a society. We were instructed to suppress our emotions, creativity, funny thoughts and crazy ideas.

Introduced into China some 2,000 years ago, Buddhism has developed into the most important religion in the Chinese-speaking world. It has had three main areas of influence: literature, art and ideology. I remember how my grandmother, a devout Buddhist, got up at 3.30 a.m. and prayed for three hours before her morning exercise in the local park. She could recite by heart the important Buddhist texts the Lotus Sutra (妙法蓮華經), Nīlakantha Dhāranī (大悲咒) and Diamond Sutra (金剛經). A shorter but similar practice occurred in the afternoon. My grandmother continued her daily routine for more than fifty years until she was too frail to do so.

At home I was under the influence of Buddhism, and at school I was told to follow Confucianism strictly, but as a rebellious girl aged nine I immersed myself in the philosophy of Taoism, which dates back to the 3rd century BCE. I studied the ancient texts I-Ching and Tao-Te Ching and the teachings of Chuang Tzu, and believed in the concepts of Wu-Wei (無爲/无为; meaning 'acts without effort') and naturalness. To attain naturalness, one needs to free oneself from desire and appreciate simplicity.

The development of Taoism over the centuries has sometimes been besmirched by charlatans peddling alchemy, life elixirs and talismans. Taoism as a religion, distinct from Taoism as a philosophy, has temples, monasteries, priests and ceremonies, and gods and goddesses of all kinds for believers to worship. Taoism's rich palette of sacrament and ritual makes it more appealing to many people than other religions.

In many parts of the Chinese-speaking world, Taoism and Buddhism are mixed with mythology and other folk religions and philosophy. Ch'an Buddhism (also called Zen), in particular, has many beliefs in common with philosophical Taoism.

Let's explore further

More ways to say 'queen'

后 queen/empress (hou⁴)

The wife of the 'king' 王 is a 'queen' 王后 (wang² hou⁴), and the wife of an 'emperor' 皇 (huang²) – a combination of 'white' 白 + 'king' 王 – is an 'empress' 皇后 (huang² hou⁴).

Although 女王 (see p. 80) and 王后 both mean 'queen', there is a subtle difference between them. 王后 means 'queen consort', the wife of the king, when the king is the ruler of a kingdom. 女王 normally indicates a female ruler of a kingdom.

During the simplification process that began in 1949 (see p. 18), the meaning of 后 was extended to represent 'after' or 'behind', because it has the same pronunciation as the traditional form of the character with this meaning: 後.

生女 vs. 女生; 生男 vs. 男生

Chinese is fun and easy. Remember 'birth' 生 (see p. 40)? When it is used as a verb, it can mean 'to give birth'. 生女 means 'to give birth to a girl' and 生男 means 'to give birth to a boy'. It's simple!

How about 生子? Although the literal meaning of 子 is 'boy', the extended meaning could be 'child' or 'children'. So when we are not sure about the sex of a baby, we can use 生子 to avoid being specific. In the case that we are certain about giving birth to a boy, 生子 and 生男 are sometimes interchangeable.

When 生 is used as a noun, it can mean 'life' or 'livelihood'. 一生 (literally, 'one life') represents a 'lifetime' (see p. 41). Traditionally, 生 was also used to refer to living things. The character was then expanded to mean 'scholar' or 'student'. So when you make the phrase 'female student', we get 'girls' 女生. And by adding 'male' to 生, we build the phrase 'boys' 男生.

女生 girls (nü³ sheng¹)

男生 boys (nan² sheng¹)

Unusual characters: 'to get angry' 嬲 and 'to flirt' 嫐

嬲 to get angry (niao³)

This character is a combination of 'male' 男 + 'female' 女 + 'male' 男. When two men fight over a woman, they are bound to become angry. 嬲 also means 'to pester' or 'to quarrel'. It is used more often in Cantonese than in other dialects.

嫐 to flirt (nao³)

This character is a combination of 'female' 女 + 'male' 男 + 'female' 女. When a man is surrounded by two women, he is flirting with both of them. Again, this character is used more frequently in Cantonese than in other dialects.

CHAPTER 4

NATURE & WEATHER

山 mountain (shan[1])

In oracle-bone inscriptions, this character depicted three mountain peaks. These peaks are still evident in the three vertical lines in the present form of the character.

川 river (chuan[1])

There are a few characters in Chinese that have remained relatively unchanged since ancient times. The character 川, which means 'river', is one such example; it's always been written as three slightly wavy lines. Sure, the modern version has been straightened up a bit, but we can still see a slight bend in the left-hand stroke. You can think of this particular stroke as a bend in the river, if that helps you remember it!

云 cloud (yun²)

The earliest form of this character in oracle-bone inscriptions depicted a talking mouth with breath coming out of it. It means 'to say' or 'to speak'. The two horizontal lines at the top of the character represent the mouth, while the bottom part indicates the breath.

This character has also come to mean 'cloud', since its pronunciation is the same as the traditional character for 'cloud' 雲, which depicts a condensed version of 'rain' (see right) on top.

雨 rain (yu³)

In its ancient form, this character comprised only two elements: a horizontal line (一) represented the sky, while underneath the sky there were a few drops that symbolized rain. In the modern form of the character, the horizontal line of the sky and the water drops remain, and the component 冂 has been added, making 雨.

雷 thunder (lei²)

This character is a combination of a very condensed version of 'rain' 雨 and 'field' 田 (tian²). To remember this compound, you can imagine a thunderstorm in ancient China, with acres of farmland being drenched with rain and flashes of thunder lighting up the sky as farmers slog through the mud towards shelter. What a dramatic image!

雪 snow (xue³)

As we have already seen with the character for 'thunder' and the traditional form of the character for 'cloud', the building block 'rain' 雨 is often used to form characters indicating weather or natural forces. The ancient Chinese perceived snow to be 'feathers' 羽 (yu³) falling from the sky. These days, 彐 is used to represent feather-like snowflakes. I like to imagine 彐 as a shovel for clearing up snow on the driveway.

電 lightning/ electricity (dian⁴)

The ancient form of this character looked nothing like its modern version; it used to look like a lightning bolt striking the ground. Although the original form of the character is no longer evident, its meaning has been retained. In addition to 'lightning', it is very commonly used to mean 'electricity'. The simplified form of the character is 电.

气 air (qi⁴)

In oracle-bone inscriptions, this character comprised three horizontal lines, and meant 'cloud vapour' or 'light, thin cloud'. In seal inscriptions, the top two lines remained the same, but the third line became an upside-down 'L'. The meaning has been extended to refer to 'air', 'steam' or 'vital energy'. This is the simplified form of the character; the traditional form is 氣, with 'rice' 米 (see p. 206) inside 'air'. The martial art based on the flow of energy inside the human body is known as Qigong 氣功/气功 (qi⁴ gong¹).

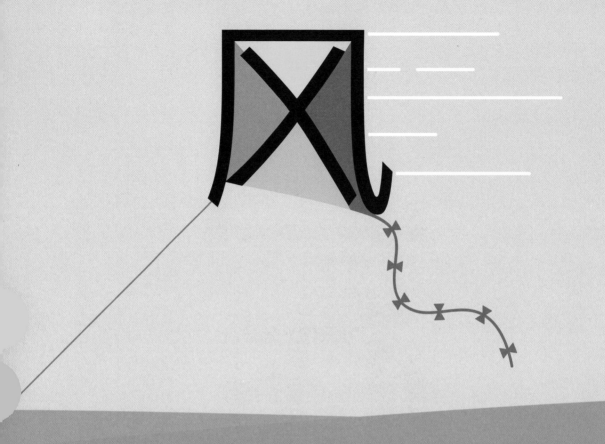

风 wind (feng[1])

The outer part (几) of this character looks like a
sail to me, and I like to think the inner part (乂) is
a sailboat mast. A sailboat needs the breeze to get
it moving, and that's how I remember the meaning
of the character – 'wind'. This is the simplified form;
the traditional form is 風.

The phrase 大风 (big + wind; da[4] feng[1]) means
'strong wind'.

Part of my name, 'Lan' 嵐 (lan[2]), is a combination of
'mountain' 山 and 'wind' 風. It means 'the mist in the
mountains'. 'Shao' 曉 (xiao[3]) means 'dawn'. So I'm
'the mist in the mountains at dawn'!

石 stone (shi²)

The character for 'stone' looks like a square-shaped stone (口) under a cliff (丁). The phrase 石頭 (simplified form: 石头; shi² tou) is widely used to mean 'stone' as well. 頭/头 means 'head' (see p. 142).

The phrase 大石 (da⁴ shi²) literally means a 'big rock'.

This character is also a common Chinese surname, pronounced 'Shi'.

雨林 rainforest
(yu³ lin²)

rain + woods = rainforest

风雨 wind and rain (feng¹ yu³)

wind + rain

The phrase 大风雨 (da⁴ feng¹ yu³) means a 'big storm with strong wind and heavy rain'. It's raining and blowing!

风光 scene/ to be well off (feng¹ guang¹)

wind + light = scene/ to be well off

The translation of this phrase depends on the context. When it is used to describe nature or the surroundings, it means 'scene' or 'view'; when it is used to describe a person, it means 'well off' or 'well regarded'.

rain　　　　woods

rainforest

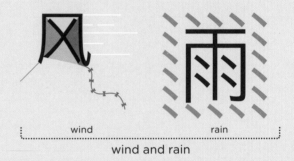

wind　　　　rain

wind and rain

wind　　　　light

scene/to be well off

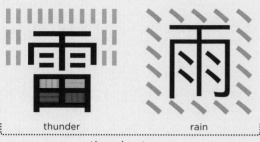

thunder · rain

thunderstorm

big · snow

heavy snow

雪

snow · person

snowman

雷雨
thunderstorm
(lei² yu³)

thunder + rain = thunderstorm

A thunderstorm usually comes with heavy rain, so this phrase is formed by 'thunder' and 'rain'. Add 'big' in front of 'thunderstorm', and we have a 'heavy thunderstorm' **大雷雨** (da⁴ lei² yu³).

大雪 heavy snow
(da⁴ xue³)

big + snow = heavy snow

'Big snow' is very heavy snow! And what do we do when there's a **大风雪** (da⁴ feng¹ xue³)? We run for our lives; it's a snowstorm!

雪人 snowman
(xue³ ren²)

snow + person = snowman

水電 water and electricity
(shui³ dian⁴)

water + electricity

Your utility bills are called 水電費 (simplified form: 水电费; shui³ dian⁴ fei⁴), which literally means 'water electricity expense'.

光電
photoelectric
(guang¹ dian⁴)

light + electricity = photoelectric

'Photoelectric' refers to electricity produced by a beam of light, so it makes sense that these two elements are used to form the phrase for 'photoelectric'.

電子 electron
(dian⁴ zi³)

electricity + small thing = electron

Electricity is generated by the flow of tiny particles called electrons around a circuit.

water   lightning/electricity

water and electricity

light   lightning/electricity

photoelectric

lightning/electricity   son/small thing

electron

sky   air

weather

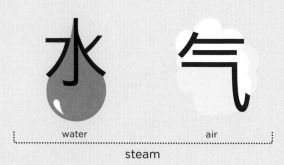

water   air

steam

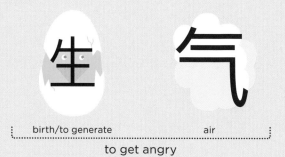

birth/to generate   air

to get angry

天气 weather
(tian¹ qi⁴)

sky + air = weather

The ancient Chinese were remarkably perceptive about nature, and the Chinese language reflects their observations. A good example is the phrase 天气: our ancestors learned that the weather is affected by how the air moves in the sky, so the phrase for 'weather' is formed by 'sky' and 'air'. This is the simplified form of the phrase; the traditional form is 天氣.

水气 steam
(shui³ qi⁴)

water + air = steam

This is the simplified form of the phrase; the traditional form is 水氣.

生气 to get angry
(sheng¹ qi⁴)

to generate + air/steam = to get angry

When 生 is used as a verb, it can mean 'to generate'. When someone is generating a lot of 'steam' 气, they are getting pretty angry. This is the simplified form of the phrase; the traditional form is 生氣.

Let's explore further

What is Feng Shui?

A few years ago, I was looking for a house to buy in central London. When the estate agent showed me a particular property, I took out my phone and, using the compass app, checked the orientation of each room. The agent was curious. 'I'm working out the Feng Shui,' I explained. There was an awkward silence. The agent must have thought I was either superstitious or paranoid. In fact, my actions were entirely reasonable. By being aware of the orientation of the house and each room within it, I know how the sunlight will enter every day of the year. I know the direction in which the wind might blow in different seasons. I can work out whether or not the house is energy-efficient. I won't go into the complicated theory behind the study of Feng Shui (which is sometimes known as the 'art of placement'), but it is a practical way of understanding and appreciating the harmony between people and their environment.

Feng is 'wind' and Shui is 'water'; together they make 風水/风水 (feng[1] shui[3]). We may associate Feng Shui with interior design (it offers useful guidance on lighting, energy preservation, ventilation and comfort), but for thousands of years the Chinese have used Feng Shui principles in urban planning, agriculture and architecture. In ancient times, a ruler would consult Feng Shui masters before deciding the location of a new capital, settlements and fortresses. They had to consider the supply of food and water, the effects of heat and cold, the likelihood of floods and storms, the position of roads to connect to the rest of the kingdom, and any military advantage in defending their people.

Before the invention of the magnetic compass, Feng Shui masters were experts in astronomy; they studied the alignment of the stars in order to decide where to build homes. Recent research has indicated that over six thousand years ago the dwellings of the ancient Bampo civilization were sited so that they gained maximum heat from the sun. Since that time, Feng Shui has developed into a complex theory influencing the daily lives of billions of people. There have been numerous schools of thought over the years. While they all have followed the same general principles, inevitably some have adapted contradictory practices, some more extreme than others. However, we should not dismiss the value of their knowledge and wisdom. After all, if you gathered together a group of Western-educated economists, they would probably all hold different theories. So why not be open-minded and see what we can learn from our ancestors!

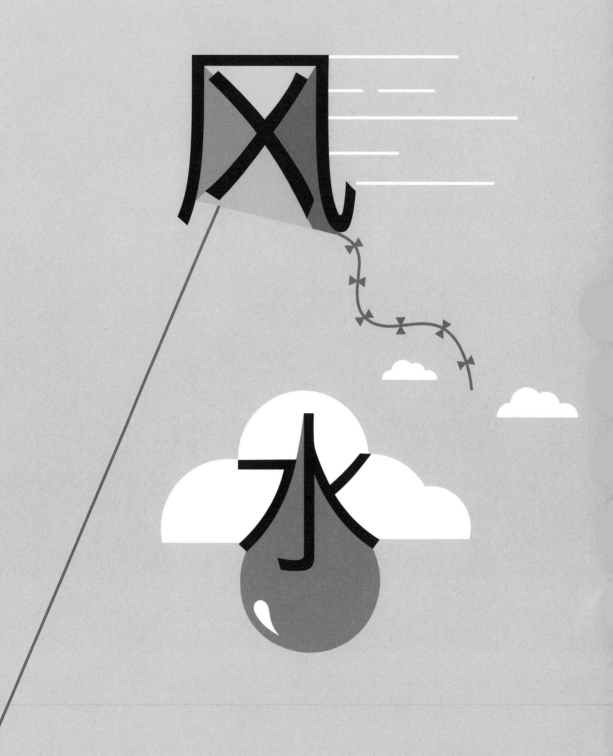

馬

鳥

犬

鸡

羊

CHAPTER 5

ANIMALS

牛 cow (niu²)

The original form of this character meant 'ox' or 'cattle', and depicted the face of an ox with upward-pointing horns. In time, the strokes depicting the horns became a left-falling stroke and a horizontal stroke, and the character came to mean 'cow'.

牛 is the form of the character used as a component in certain compounds.

熊 bear (xiong²)

In ancient scripts, this character depicted a bear with sharp teeth and claws. For thousands of years across China, the bear, along with the tiger (see p. 116), has been perceived as a symbol of bravery. The awful tradition of considering bear paws a delicacy is finally being challenged, but illegal hunting and smuggling remain a serious problem. Bear bile is widely used as a potent ingredient in traditional medicine, and caged bears suffer a painful extraction process.

馬 horse (ma³)

In the illustration, you can see the horse is on its side, and that's how our ancestors designed this character. The simplified form is 马.

As a building block, 馬 appears in some very useful compounds, including 嗎 (ma; a question indicator, used at the end of a sentence – see p. 135) and 媽 (ma¹; mum – see p. 71).

羊 sheep (yang²)

In oracle-bone script, this character depicted a sheep's face with a pair of horns. Over time, the face became the two lower horizontal strokes (the third stroke used to be part of the horns). Today the character represents the goat-antelope subfamily of mammals, and is used in phrases to refer to specific animals: e.g. 'mountain' + 'sheep' = 'mountain goat' 山羊 (shan¹ yang²); 'soft' + 'sheep' = 'sheep' 綿羊 (mian² yang²). 羊 is also used as a component in different compounds.

蛇 snake (she[2])

Take a close look at the illustration above. The character for 'snake' is a combination of 'bug' 虫 (chong[2]) and 它 (ta[1]). In ancient scripts, 它 meant 'snake', but the character was later borrowed to represent 'it'. To differentiate between the two, a 'bug' was added next to 它 to show 'snake'.

兔 rabbit (tu[4])

In oracle-bone script, the character for 'rabbit' depicted a rabbit on its side. Over time, rabbit features have been added. I like to remember the character by thinking that the top part (ク) represents the rabbit's long ears, with its eyes in the middle and its strong back legs at the bottom of the character. And how about that little dot on the right side of the character? It's the rabbit's tail, of course – so cute!

鸡 chicken (ji[1])

This is the simplified form of 'chicken'; the traditional form is 雞, which, according to its etymology, depicts a huge bird 鳥 (see p. 111) that is tied up and teased (奚) for people's pleasure. Archaeologists have found fossilized chicken bones in northeastern China dating to around 5400 BCE, although they believe domestication was originally for the purpose of cockfighting. Chicken is an increasingly popular source of protein, but in general Chinese people prefer brown meat to white.

鼠 rat (shu[3])

This character is simply the pictograph of a rat. It may be rather a strange image, but imagine a rat wearing a nice top and a pair of trousers with a four-dotted pattern!

In Chinese, there is no significant difference between mice and rats, so they share this character.

犬 dog (quan³)

On its own, 犬 means 'dog', but you will usually see this character in its compound form, 犭. When you see 犭, you know those are characters related to dog-like mammals, such as 'fox' 狸 (li²), 'wolf' 狼 (lang²), 'lion' 獅 (shi¹) or 'jackal' 豺 (chai²), or primates, such as 'monkey' 猴 (see p. 110), 'ape' 猿 (yuan²) or 'gorilla' 猩 (xing¹). It seems that the ancient Chinese people did not rationalize animals in the same way as do modern Western biologists.

犭 is also sometimes used as a building block for descriptive compounds:

'dog' 犭 + 'king' 王 = 'crazy' 狂 (kuang²)

'dog' 犭 + 'tough' 艮 (gen³) = 'ferocious'/'cruel' 狠 (hen³)

'dog' 犭 + 'prosperous' 昌 (chang¹) = 'reckless' 猖 (chang¹)

狗 dog (gou³)

The more commonly used character for 'dog' is a combination of 犭, indicating the meaning, and 'sentence' 句 (ju⁴), indicating the pronunciation. This is the phono-semantic, or pictophonetic, method of building characters (see p. 15).

豕 swine/pig (shi³)

The original form of this character featured a long snout, a big belly, hooves and a tail. In modern Chinese, 豕 is rarely used alone; you'll typically see it in such compound characters as 'pig' 豬 (see below), 'young pig' 豚 (tun²), 'elephant' 象 (see p. 113) or 'home' 家 (jia¹; depicting a pig underneath a roof). As in the case of the character for 'dog', this is an example of the discrepancy between the formation of Chinese characters and modern biological classification.

豬 pig (zhu¹)

豬 is much more commonly used to refer to 'pig'. It follows the same phono-semantic, or pictophonetic, principle as 'dog' (see opposite), in that 豕 indicates the meaning ('semantic'/'picto-'), and 'those who'/'that which' 者 (zhe³) indicates the pronunciation ('phono-'/ 'phonetic'). During the simplification process that began in 1949 (see p. 18), 豕 became 犭, making the character for 'pig' 猪.

If we add 'mountain' and 'pig' together, we get the phrase 'wild boar' 山豬 (shan¹ zhu¹; see p. 214).

猴 monkey (hou²)

This character is a combination of 'dog', indicating the meaning, and 'lord' 侯 (hou²), indicating the pronunciation. By now you may have noticed that the majority of Chinese characters are phono-semantic. When life was simple, primitive pictographs were dominant. To convey more complex meanings, our Chinese ancestors started building characters by using the phono-semantic method. It was an effective way of increasing the number of symbols quickly.

貓 cat (mao¹)

This character is a combination of 豸 (zhi⁴) on the left, indicating the meaning, and 'bud' 苗 (see p. 204) on the right, indicating the pronunciation. 豸 is a legendary creature in Chinese, Japanese and Korean mythology. Some ancient literature refers to it as 'feetless bugs'. The simplified form of 'cat' is 猫, where 豸 has been replaced with 犭, representing dog-like animals.

If we add 'mountain' and 'cat' together, we get the phrase 'lynx' 山貓 (shan¹ mao¹).

鳥 bird (niao³)

In oracle-bone script, this character looked just like a bird. Over time, however, the lines that made up the bird's talons, beak and tail feathers became more geometric. In simplified Chinese, the character has become even further removed from the original form, with the small strokes at the bottom turning into a single straight line: 鸟.

This character looks similar to 'horse' 馬/马. The main difference is the small stroke on top of 鳥/鸟.

鴨 duck (ya¹)

This character is a combination of 'armour' 甲 (jia³) and 'bird'. Did the ancient Chinese really think that ducks were birds with a shield? Maybe, but actually it's another good example of a phono-semantic character: 甲 is phonetic and 鳥 semantic.

Duck is a popular food in China and Taiwan. The first recorded recipe for the signature dish 'Peking duck' 北京烤鴨 (bei³ jing¹ kao³ ya¹) is in an imperial Chinese cookbook of 1330.

毛 hair/fur (mao²)

Originally, this character depicted the hair or fur of animals, and the lines in its original form were more curved. In its modern form, the lines are much straighter. 毛 can be used to describe human body hair, but not the hair growing on the head; for that, we use 髮/发 (see p. 143). When 毛 is used as an adjective, it can mean 'rough' – as in a surface that is uneven.

Mao is also a common Chinese surname. The most famous person from the Mao family must be Mao Zedong (毛澤東/毛泽东; mao² ze² dong¹).

....

羊毛 sheep's wool (yang² mao²)

sheep + hair

馬毛 horse hair (ma³ mao²)

horse + hair

兔毛 rabbit fur (tu⁴ mao²)

rabbit + hair/fur

象 elephant
(xiang⁴)

This character originally depicted the side view of an elephant, including its trunk and tusks. In its modern form, the outline of an elephant is less clear. However, the trunk and tusks are still distinct; observe those three lines falling right to left. You can see the 'pig' 豕 building block in the lower half of the character.

The Chinese zodiac

As in the case of most ancient myths from around the world, there are many versions of the story of the origins of the Chinese zodiac, with its twelve-year cycle. This is the version I heard most often when I was a young child.

Once upon a time, when most people were poorly educated, there was no effective way of recording the time, such as years, months, days or hours. The Jade Emperor decided to use common animals to form a calender, thus developing an easy way to allow ordinary folks to understand the concept of time. Yet even the clever Jade Emperor could not settle on the choice and sequence of the animals. He declared that on his birthday he would hold a race to cross the river, and announced that the new calendar would be based on the rank of the top twelve animals in the race.

All the animals were excited, and began to prepare for the competition. However, some animals were not good at swimming. Two close friends, Cat and Rat, went to ask for a favour from Cow, who was known to be kind and gentle. Cow agreed to take them across the river. In the early morning on the day of the competition, Rat could not wake up Cat, who was sleeping soundly. Cow urged Rat to give up and start the race. (In another version of the story, devious Rat deliberately fails to wake up Cat.) Just before the finishing line, Cow started shaking his head, trying to get rid of Rat, who was balancing on his horns. It was a competition, after all. Rat was thrown on to a branch and then bounced across the finishing line, becoming the race winner. (A different version of the story has sneaky Rat jumping ahead as soon as Cow takes him over the river.) The race finished, and the top twelve winners were announced (see the order below). Cat, having missed the race altogether, was bitter and blamed Rat for destroying the trust between friends, and so started chasing him. This is when vindictive Cat and guilty Rat became enemies.

     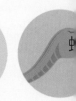

Throughout my childhood I heard more than ten different versions of the story of the Chinese zodiac, with small or significant variations. We know that cats had not been introduced to China at the time the zodiac was established.

For thousands of years, the twelve-part zodiac has influenced daily life in China on many levels. The earliest literature that mentions the zodiac dates back to the Qin dynasty (c. 220 BCE), with a small difference being that the Dragon is a Bug in that version. The twelve animals became the labelling system for the calendar (years and months) and the time (in ancient China, every two hours represented one unit in a day). Theories have been developed to predict one's personality, fortune and major life decisions, such as career and marriage, on the basis of the characteristics attributed to each animal of the zodiac.

Millions of Chinese people firmly believe the happiness (or unhappiness) of their marriage is determined by the 'perfect match' of a couple's zodiac. For example, a Dragon matches a Rat, Monkey and Chicken auspiciously, but matches a Cow, Rabbit, Dog or another Dragon adversely. The belief system extends to every kind of human relationship, such as between parents and their children, and among siblings, colleagues and friends. The Chinese also believe that children born into a certain zodiac will have better luck and fortune than others. Having a Dragon boy is the dream of many families, as those Dragon babies will supposedly have a prosperous career and good fortune. The effect on society as a whole may be less advantageous, however. In 2012, the last year of the Dragon, the birth rate in China increased by 5 per cent on the recent annual average of 16 million births. As these children grow older, they will face fierce competition from their peers, and there will be enormous pressure on the education system, the job market and hospitals.

I'm a happy-go-lucky pig – how about you?

Let's explore further

龙 dragon (long²)

The dragon is probably the most important and symbolic animal in Chinese history. Chinese people call themselves 'the descendants of the dragon'. This legendary creature has the antlers of a deer, the head of a crocodile, the eyes of a demon, the neck of a snake, the viscera of a tortoise, the claws of a hawk, the palms of a tiger and the ears of a cow. 龙 is the simplified form of 'dragon'; the traditional form is 龍.

While the dragon often symbolizes aggression and even evil in Western culture, in China it is believed to have auspicious powers that control rainfall, storms, floods and drought. Chinese people pray to the dragon for protection and desirable weather for farming. They call the ruler of the sea 'the king of the dragon' 龍王/龙王 (long² wang²). The five-clawed dragon has been the symbol of the Emperor of China since the Zhou dynasty (c. 1046–256 BCE).

虎 tiger (hu³)

虎 is one of the pictographic characters from ancient China. When it is used as an adjective, it means 'brave'. For thousands of years nearly every part of a tiger, from its claws, bones, bile, eyes and brain to its penis, whiskers and teeth, has been used as an ingredient in traditional Chinese medicine. Although tigers were classified as globally endangered in 1986, and the international trade of tiger parts is banned, a black market still exists.

One of the first idioms many people pick up when they learn Chinese is 馬馬虎虎/马马虎虎 ('horse horse, tiger tiger'; ma³ ma hu¹ hu¹), expressing something sloppy or careless. This idiom has its origins in the belief that humans are superior to other animals.

The phrase 虎媽 (hu³ ma¹) is literally a 'tiger mother', meaning a strict or demanding mother who pushes her children to high levels of achievement. No, I'm not one of them! In fact, I'm a 'kitty mother'.

The use of gender in animals

In English terminology for animals, we have separate words to differentiate between the genders. For example, a male cow is called a 'bull', and a female is called a 'cow'; a male pig is called a 'boar', and a female is called a 'sow'.

In Chinese, it is much easier to give the gender of an animal; we just need to use two characters – 公 (gong[1]; 'male') and 母 (mu[3]; 'female') – to distinguish between the genders. Here are some examples:

cow: 牛   bull: 公牛 (male + cow)   cow: 母牛 (female + cow)

pig: 豬   boar: 公豬 (male + pig)   sow: 母豬 (female + pig)

It's important to remember that 公 and 母 are the gender descriptors for animals only. When describing the gender identity of people, we use 男 (male) and 女 (female) instead (see pp. 66–67).

Other interesting phrases

馬夫 groom (ma[3] fu[1])

horse + man = groom

Horses have long been associated with masculinity in both Eastern and Western cultures. Take, for example, the English phrase 'as strong as a horse', or any Western film! Cowboys are the quintessential manly men.

Perhaps this is the reason why the Chinese phrase referring to a keeper of horses uses 夫 (man) instead of the common 人 (person) building block. So, in addition to 'groom', 馬夫 also means 'horse keeper' or 'stableman'.

....

天馬 Pegasus (tian[1] ma[3])

sky + horse = Pegasus

This is definitely the coolest 'horse' phrase you will learn in Chinese. The ancient Greek legends surrounding this mythical winged stallion are numerous and varied, but a few stories are popularly known, including his unconventional birth: it's said that when Perseus beheaded the Gorgon Medusa, Pegasus and his brother, Chrysaor, were born from the mingling of Medusa's blood with sea foam; his father was Poseidon, the god of the sea.

Pegasus is also the name of a constellation in the northern sky. In Chinese, we use the phrase 天馬星 (tian[1] ma[3] xing[1]; 'Pegasus star') to mean 'Pegasus constellation'.

CHAPTER 6

HOW TO DESCRIBE THINGS

大 big (da⁴)

What is your first impression when you see a *rikishi* (Japanese sumo wrestler)? He is BIG! See p. 63 for more on this character.

小 small (xiao³)

In oracle-bone script, this character looked like three small dots. Then, in seal script, the three dots became three lines, and eventually the character evolved to its present form. To me, 小 resembles a kneeling man with his arms by his sides, as if he is trying to make himself as small as possible.

大小 size (da⁴ xiao³)

big + small = size

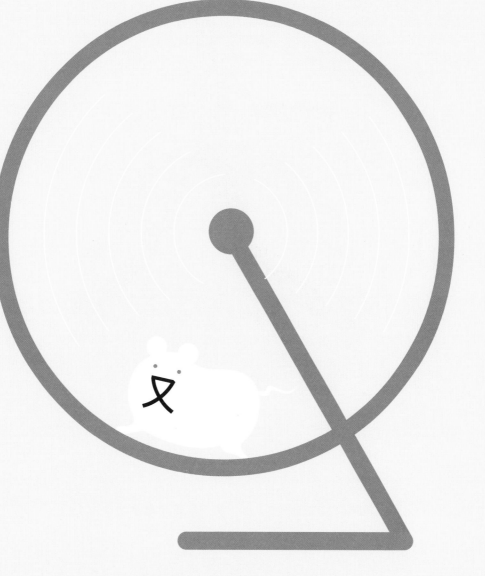

又 again (you⁴)

Originally, this character depicted a right hand and, indeed, that's what it meant. Over time, another character for 'right hand' was created (see p. 127), and so 又 evolved to mean 'again', 'also' or 'in addition'.

不 no/not (bu⁴)

According to statistics, this is the fourth most frequently used character in the Chinese language. In addition to the literal meaning 'no', 不 is essential when you are expressing something negative, in much the same way that the prefixes 'un-', 'im-', 'il-' or 'dis-' are used in English. Check out pp. 134–35, and you'll be amazed how useful 不 is, and how easily you can learn.

When this character appears in a phrase, its pronunciation varies, depending on the following character. See p. 19 and also the examples on pp. 134–35.

好 good/OK (hao³)

To say 'hello' in Chinese, we use 你好 (ni³ hao³). *Ni* is 'you', and *hao* means 'good', so we greet one another with 'You good'!

As we've seen on p. 72, 'good' is a combination of the building blocks 'woman' 女 and 'boy' 子. In ancient China, women were good only when they had given birth to a boy.

好 can also be used to mean 'OK' or 'yes'. When the character is used as an adjective, it means 'so', 'very' or 'such' ('so big', 'so beautiful', 'so long', etc.).

I definitely recommend that you list 好 as one of your Top 10 Chineasy characters.

上 up/above (shang⁴)

In oracle-bone script, the character for 'up' looked very much like the character for 'two' (二); the bottom line indicated the earth's surface, while the upper line indicated anything above the earth. It wasn't until the bronze script, when a vertical line was added, that this character came to resemble its modern form.

Besides representing such prepositions as 'up', 'above' or 'on top of' and the adjective 'upper', 上 can indicate such verbs as 'to ascend', 'to go up' or 'to climb'; see the phrases on pp. 134 and 162–63.

下 down/below (xia⁴)

The original form of the character for 'down' also resembled the character for 'two' (二); however, the upper horizontal line was longer than the lower line. The evolution of the form of this character was very similar to that of the character 上 as well.

In much the same way that 上 has various meanings, 下 has several usages besides 'down', including 'below', 'lower', 'to descend', 'to go down' and 'to get off'; see the phrases on pp. 134 and 162–63.

卡 to block (ka³)

This character is a combination of 'up' 上 and 'down' 下. When something cannot move either up or down, it is stuck; thus, the meaning of 卡 is 'to block'.

Interestingly, because of its pronunciation, which is similar to the English word, 卡 also means 'card'. So the phrase for 'birthday card' is 生日卡 (sheng¹ ri⁴ ka³).

老 old (lao³)

In oracle-bone inscriptions, this character depicted an old man with long hair bent over a cane.

老人 old person (lao³ ren²; old + person)

老太太 old lady (lao³ tai⁴ tai; old + lady)

老友 old friend (lao³ you³; old + friend; see p. 187 for 'friend')

老鳥 'veteran'/'someone with much experience' (lao³ niao³; old + bird)

Another character meaning 'old' or 'ancient' is 古 (gu³). Can you see 'ten' 十 on top of 'mouth' 口?

左 left (zuo³)

In oracle-bone inscriptions, this character depicted a left hand. Later, its meaning became simply 'left'; however, the trace of 'left hand' can still be seen in the modern form of the character, in the component ナ.

右 right (you[4])

The character for 'right' has an ancient origin similar to that of the character for 'left', 左; originally, the character 右 depicted a right hand. The component 'mouth' 口 (see p. 138) was added later at the bottom, and because of 口, I remember this character by thinking that, as a right-handed person, I use my 'right' 右 hand when I'm eating.

中 middle (zhong[1])

Originally, this character depicted a flagpole standing in the middle of a peace zone. In ancient China, when a war began, both sides would establish a peace zone and put up a flagpole to indicate the centre of the zone. In the modern form of the character, the flagpole has been simplified to become a vertical line.

中 is also an abbreviation of 'China' (see p. 174), as Chinese people believed they were at the centre of the universe.

When pronounced as 'zhong", with a high-pitched tone, the character means 'middle' or 'centre'. When pronounced as 'zhong[4]', with a sharp-falling tone, the character means 'to hit the target'.

平 equal (ping²)

This character is a combination of 'shield' 干 (gan¹) and 丷, the compound form of the character for 'eight'. It also means 'gentle', 'flat', 'even' or 'level'.

好平 so flat (hao³ ping²)

so + equal/flat

不平 not flat/uneven (bu⁴ ping²)

not + equal/flat = uneven

半 half (ban⁴)

Appropriately, the character for 'half' has a symmetrical form. If you split the character in half lengthways, each half will be a mirror image of the other.

半百 fifty (ban⁴ bai³)

half + hundred = fifty

Half of one hundred is fifty. Easy! 半百 is often a subtle way to describe someone's age.

'Fifty' can also be written as 五十 (wu³ shi²; see p. 24).

一半 one half (yi² ban⁴)

one + half

In some contexts, this phrase can also be used to mean simply 'half'.

一点半 half past one (yi⁴ dian³ ban⁴)

one + o'clock + half = half past one

In Chinese, the pattern for telling the time at half past the hour is: the hour + 'o'clock' 点 + 'half' 半.

So, 'half past two' is 'two' 二 + 'o'clock' 点 + 'half' 半, and so on.

長 long/to grow
(chang[2]/zhang[3])

Originally, this character depicted a person with long hair. In ancient China, men used to let their hair grow long. They weren't allowed to cut it, because hair was considered to be something given to children by their parents, and so it was treated as a precious gift.

In this way, the character came to mean 'long' or 'lengthy'. In Chinese, the famous Great Wall is called 長城 (chang[2] cheng[2]) because it is so long.

When you pronounce 長 as 'zhang[3]', it means 'to grow', as in 'to grow physically' or 'to develop particular features'. This second meaning makes sense when you consider that as the men of ancient China grew their hair long, they also grew physically. The simplified form is 长.

太長 'too long'

好長 'very long'

不長 'not long'

....

長大 to grow up
(zhang[3] da[4])

to grow + big
= to grow up

When we grow up, we tend to grow larger physically.

高 tall/high (gao¹)

A rocket shoots high, so this illustration expresses the character's meaning well: 'tall' or 'high'. 高 can be used to refer to the height (vertical length) of an object or the height of a person.

太高 'too tall/high'

好高 'very tall/high'

不高 'not tall/high'

長高 to grow tall (zhang³ gao¹)

to grow + tall

長不高 unable to grow tall (zhang³ bu⁴ gao¹)

to grow + not + tall = unable to grow tall

In Chinese, when we want to say that someone is unable to do or be something, the negative character 不 ('not') is placed between the verb (長) and the adjective (高). The phrase below follows the same pattern.

長不大
unable to grow up (zhang³ bu⁴ da⁴)

to grow + not + big = unable to grow up

長好高
to grow very tall (zhang³ hao³ gao¹)

to grow + very + tall

Let's explore further

Neither A nor B: 不 A 不 B

'不 A 不 B' is an interesting Chinese phrase, used in a similar way to the English phrase 'neither A nor B'. As the examples below show, 'A' and 'B' can be replaced by different characters to form different phrases.

不大不小 (bu⁴ da⁴ bu⁴ xiao³)

[literally] not big not small

When something is 'neither too big nor too small', it is the perfect size. Depending on the context, sometimes we use 不大不小 to describe someone's age, especially teenagers or young people in their early twenties.

不左不右 (bu⁴ zuo³ bu⁴ you⁴)

[literally] not left not right

This phrase means 'neither left nor right'. It can be used in a political context.

不上不下 (bu⁴ shang⁴ bu⁴ xia⁴)

[literally] not up not down

This phrase means 'neither up nor down', implying 'stuck in the middle'. It is often used to describe someone's career.

不三不四 (bu⁴ san¹ bu⁴ si⁴)

[literally] not three not four

This is a very common expression meaning 'dubious'. When we use 不三不四 to describe people, it means 'those dodgy (or shady) characters'.

Chinese intensifiers/modifiers

In English, we use such words as 'very', 'so' or 'extremely' to make descriptive words – adjectives – stronger. In grammatical terms, these words are called 'intensifiers'.

In this chapter, I've introduced the Chinese intensifier 好 (hao³), which means 'so' or 'very' when placed before an adjective. And we've also already seen that 太 (tai⁴) can mean 'extremely' or 'so' (see p. 63). Here are some other common Chinese intensifiers:

很 'very' (hen³) – this character can also be used as a neutral 'filler'; see below.

真 'really' (zhen¹)

最 'most' (zui⁴)

特別 'especially' (te⁴ bie²)

比較/比较 'relatively/comparatively' (bi³ jiao⁴)

有一點/有一点 'a little' (you³ yi⁴ dian³)

很 sometimes carries no particular meaning, especially in sentences that express feelings or status. For example, 我很好 (wo³ hen³ hao³) means 'I'm fine.' 我 is 'I', 好 is 'fine' or 'good', and 很 acts as a filler word, with no meaning in particular.

Asking yes/no questions in Chinese

In Chinese, there are several ways to ask a yes/no question. I will teach you the two most common ways. One way is to add the question indicator 嗎 (ma) to the end of a sentence. For example:

你高。 'You are tall.' (ni³ gao¹)

你高嗎？ 'Are you tall?' (ni³ gao¹ ma?)

The order of the characters is the same in the two sentences above, but the second sentence ends with the question indicator 嗎, which turns an affirmative sentence into an interrogative one.

In this way, you can easily build many questions. For example: 王太太好嗎？ 'Is Mrs Wang well?' (wang² tai⁴ tai hao³ ma?)

Another way to form a yes/no question is to use the negative character 不 ('not'; bu⁴) to create a positive/negative phrase. We take the adjective or verb from an affirmative sentence and build a phrase as follows: adjective (or verb) + 不 + adjective (or verb).

For example:

你高不高？ 'Are you tall?' (ni³ gao¹ bu⁴ gao¹?)

[literally] You tall or not tall?

水星大不大？ 'Is Mercury big?' (shui³ xing¹ da⁴ bu⁴ da⁴?)

[literally] Mercury big or not big?

你是不是王太太？ 'Are you Mrs Wang?' (ni³ shi⁴ bu⁴ shi⁴ wang² tai⁴ tai?)

[literally] You are or not are Mrs Wang?

It's necessary to add a question mark whether you are using 嗎 or 不. And note that the Chinese full stop is a small circle that takes the space of one character (see the first example above).

CHAPTER 7

HEALTH & WELL-BEING

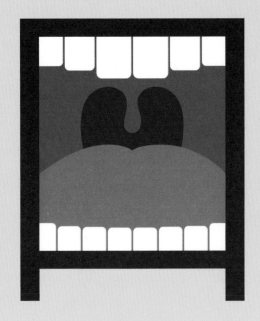

口 mouth (kou³)

As our illustration clearly shows, the character 口 means 'mouth'. It's simply a square shape; please ignore the two little legs at the bottom, because they are the result of the font we are using in this book!

口 is a very useful building block. For example, if we add 'no' 不 on top of 'mouth', we make 'to deny' 否 (fou³). If we put 'woman' 女 next to 'mouth', she is 'obedient' 如 (ru²) to her father's and her husband's commands. In addition to 'to obey', 如 has been extended to mean 'according to' or 'as if'. What's the natural reaction if a baby puts 'soil' 土 in his mouth? He 'spits' 吐 (tu³) the soil out; 吐 means 'to spit'.

'Mouth' is easily confused with the building block 'to surround' 囗 (wei²). However, the character for 'to surround' never appears alone, so if you see 口 by itself, it always means 'mouth'. In addition, another building block always appears inside 'to surround'. For example, 'to return' 回 (hui²) is a combination of 'mouth' and 'to surround'. When a 'person' 人 is trapped, he is a 'prisoner' 囚 (qiu²).

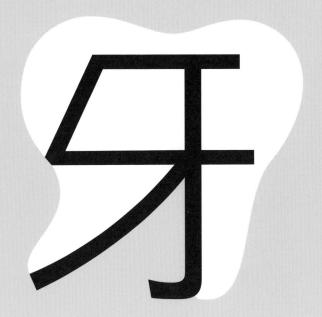

牙 tooth (ya²)

In bronze script, the character for 'tooth' resembled the upper and lower sets of teeth biting together. In Chinese, the phrase for 'molar' is 大牙 (da⁴ ya²; big + tooth), 'canine' is 犬牙 (quan³ ya²; dog + tooth) and 'incisor' is 門牙 (men² ya²; door + tooth).

牙 is interchangeable with the character 齒 (chi³). Even without an illustration, I can see a big mouth with two rows of sharp teeth.

耳 ear (er³)

耳 is one of the ancient Chinese pictographs; the original form looked just like an ear. You can imagine that the opening of the ear is the outer box (口), the cartilage inside the ear is the horizontal lines (二) inside the box, and the earlobe is on the lower right (十).

左耳 left ear (zuo³ er³)

右耳 right ear (you⁴ er³)

The 'king' 王 is the 'ear' 耳 and the 'mouth' 口 of the 'saint': 聖 (sheng⁴). This character conveys the idea of articulating and spreading the wisdom of the saint and listening to the voice of the divine.

An 'ear' 耳 and an 'eye' 目 (see opposite) together make the phrase for 'intelligence' or 'spy': 耳目 (er³ mu⁴). When you have eyes and ears everywhere, you collect intelligence.

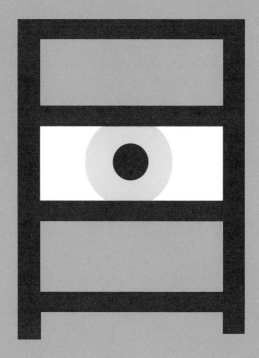

目 eye (mu⁴)

Originally, this character was a pictograph of a human eye and, in comparison to its modern form, it was rotated 90 degrees in a clockwise direction and had curvier lines. As the Chinese language evolved, many characters that were primarily circular or had many curved lines were straightened out in order to make them easier to write. Further examples are 'mouth' 口 and 'hand' 手 (see p. 146).

If you add a dot on top of 'eye', it means 'self' or 'oneself': 自 (zi⁴). It's easy to imagine that we look into ourselves with our eyes.

目光 vision/gaze (mu⁴ guang¹; eye + light)

头 head (tou²)

Many simplified characters were not introduced until 1949, when the Communist Party took control of mainland China. However, the character for 'head' is a different story. The modern simplified version, 头, which looks like two dots on top of 'big' 大, has been in use for thousands of years.

The traditional form is 頭. Sometimes the traditional form of a character offers more clues to its meaning than the simplified form. But in this instance, I think the simplified character is easier to remember.

头 is sometimes used to mean 'individual' or 'single':

石头 individual stone (shi² tou; stone + head; see also p. 95)

骨头 individual bone (gu³ tou; bone + head; see p. 148 for 'bone')

The phrase 头大 (tou² da⁴) can refer literally to someone with a 'big head'. Or it can be used figuratively to mean that you don't know how to deal with a difficult challenge, as in 'My head is swimming.'

发 hair (fa³)

发 is the simplified form of two very useful characters: 'hair' 髮 and 'to start' 發. The traditional character for 'hair' (髮) is phono-semantic: 'hair' 髟 (biao¹) indicates the meaning, while 犮 (ba²) indicates the pronunciation. 犮 once used to mean 'dog', but in modern Chinese it appears only as a component in compound characters to indicate the sound.

When 发 is used as a verb, it is pronounced as 'fa¹'. Its traditional form (發) is probably one of the most loved characters in the Chinese language. 發 originally represented the sound of a bowstring when

shooting an arrow, then its meaning was extended to indicate 'to start' or 'to depart'. Later on, the meaning expanded again, to describe someone achieving incredible success. The character for 'eight' 八 (ba¹) is considered lucky because it sounds similar to 发/發.

发生 to happen (fa¹ sheng¹; to start + birth)

发明 to invent (fa¹ ming²; to start + brightness)

发炎 to inflame (fa¹ yan²; to start + inflammation)

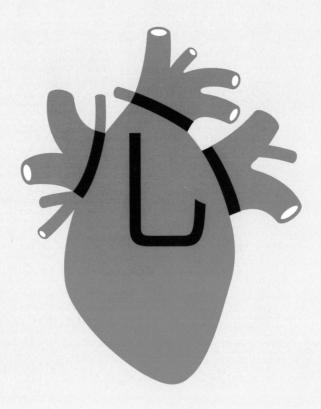

心 heart (xin¹)

The original form of this character depicted a heart. With the aid of our illustration, you can still see how the shorter, slanted strokes represent the main arteries carrying blood away from the heart to the rest of the body.

Wherever your heart (心) is centred (中) is where your 'loyalty' 忠 (zhong¹) lies. Wherever your heart (心) is cultivated (田) shows what you are thinking about; 思 (si¹) means 'to think'. When you are trapped behind a door (門), it's 'stuffy' and you're 'bored' 悶 (men⁴).

忄 is the form of the character used as a component in certain compounds. Typically, if you see 心 or 忄 in a compound character, you know its meaning has something to do with emotions or the act of thinking. For example, your heart is 'dead' 亡 (wang²) when you are 'busy' 忙 (mang²).

舌 tongue (she²)

舌 is one of the ancient Chinese pictographs, representing a forked tongue emerging from a mouth.

The phrase 口舌 (kou³ she²) can refer to its literal meaning, 'mouth and tongue', but it is also used to mean 'to argue' or 'to dispute'.

長舌 (chang² she²; long + tongue) means 'gossip'; when someone has a very long tongue, he or she is a 'blabbermouth'.

舌尖 (she² jian¹) can mean 'tip of the tongue', as the literal translation suggests, but it is also used to express 'taste'. There is a popular TV series in China called *A Bite of China* 舌尖上的中国 (she² jian¹ shang⁴ de zhong¹ guo²), which is about the history of food throughout the country.

手 hand (shou³)

In its original form, this character was an interesting depiction of the human hand. The top stroke was once a continuation of the vertical stroke, representing the middle finger. The other two horizontal strokes were once slanted upwards, and represented the other digits of the hand. I like to remember this character by comparing it to the lines on our palms.

扌 is the form of the character used as a component in certain compounds. It is known as 'the lifting hand' 提手旁 (ti² shou³ pang²). 手 becomes 扌 only when it's placed on the left side in a compound character.

When you see 扌 in a compound, the meaning is likely to be associated with actions that require the use of hands, such as 'to hit' 打 (da³), 'to steal' 扒 (pa²) and 'to carry something on your shoulders' 扛 (kang²).

左手 left hand (zuo³ shou³)

右手 right hand (you⁴ shou³)

左右手 right-hand man (zuo³ you⁴ shou³; left + right + hand)

足 foot (zu²)

The character for 'foot' originally also meant 'to levy troops'. This is logical, since the major force in an army was the infantry – the foot soldiers. (Later, another character was created to mean specifically 'to levy troops'.) The ancient symbol for 足 represented the entire leg; it is only in modern times that the character has come to mean 'foot'.

When it is used as an adjective, this character means 'sufficient' or 'ample'. To express the opposite, we use the phrase 不足 (bu⁴ zu²) to mean something is 'not enough' or 'insufficient'.

手足 siblings (shou³ zu²)

The closest people to us, genetically speaking, are probably our siblings – unless you have a clone! To express the intimacy between siblings, the phrase 'hand and foot' is used to refer to brothers and sisters. It's a very commonly used phrase and an elegant expression to know.

手口足病 hand, foot and mouth disease (shou³ kou³ zu² bing⁴; hand + mouth + foot + illness; see p. 149 for 'illness')

骨 bone (gu³)

The ancient form of the character for 'bone' was a combination of 'skull' 冎 (gua³) and the ancient compound form of 'flesh' 月; today the modern compound form of 'flesh' is used: 月 (see 'meat', p. 212). This is a typical ideogramic compound. The meaning of the character has been extended to represent 'frame' or 'framework'.

头骨 skull (tou² gu³; head + bone)

疒 to indicate illness (ne⁴)

The building block 疒 doesn't exist as a stand-alone character. It indicates illness when you see it combined with other characters. The shape of 疒 originally resembled a sick person sweating in bed.

症 disease (zheng⁴)

病 illness (bing⁴)

疾 sickness (ji²)

痛 pain (tong⁴)

疼 ache (teng²)

疲 exhausted (pi²)

瘁 weary (cui⁴)

疯 insane (feng¹)

牙痛 toothache (ya² tong⁴; tooth + pain)

心痛 heartache (xin¹ tong⁴; heart + pain)

头痛 headache (tou² tong⁴; head + pain)

大病 fatal illness (da⁴ bing⁴; big + illness)

小病 minor infection (xiao³ bing⁴; small + illness)

病人 patient (bing⁴ ren²; illness + person)

生病 to get sick (sheng¹ bing⁴; to generate + illness)

When your 'heart' 心 is 'sick' 病, you have 'heart disease' 心病 (xin¹ bing⁴). This phrase can also imply that you are paranoid or obsessed with something.

9 useful characters

Even if you know only a few building blocks, you can combine them to create
many more Chinese characters. Because there are so many fun characters I want
to share with you in this book, there is space here to list only a few examples
formed from the building blocks learned in chapters 1 to 7: 8 new compounds
and 1 new building block ('jade'); page references to the relevant building blocks
appear after each pinyin. You could actually create a few hundred new characters
and phrases from what you have learned so far – that's amazing!

朋 friend (peng²)
pp. 28, 187

本 foundation/origin (ben³)
pp. 22, 49

坐 to sit (zuo⁴)
pp. 48, 62

玉 jade (yu⁴)
p. 74

出 to get out (chu¹)
p. 88

洋 ocean/foreign (yang²)
pp. 46, 105

美 beautiful (mei³)
pp. 63, 105

吉 auspicious (ji²)
pp. 79, 138

拍 to pat/to take (pai¹)
pp. 28, 146

Let's explore further

Traditional Chinese medicine

When my first child, MuLan, was born, I was studying as a postgraduate at the University of Cambridge. I was supposed to be in class on the day she came into the world, but I made the right decision to go to the hospital that morning. MuLan was born after a complicated and dramatic 12-hour labour. Two weeks later, I returned to the dorm and resumed student life, juggling classes, seminars, exams and baby-feedings. My family and friends in Taiwan thought I was mad. Everything I did went against the fundamental principles of post-natal care in traditional Chinese medicine (TCM), according to which women should follow a strict regime and rest in bed — no showering or washing of hair, no exposure to the cold or wind, no cold food, no climbing upstairs or moving around, and no reading for at least 30 days after the birth. This is called the 'confinement process' 坐月子 (zuo^4 yue^4 zi).

I was an active, full-time student and devoted first-time mother learning a new language and taking an intensive advanced degree course in a foreign country. I broke every single confinement rule except one: no ice-cold drinks or food, a lesson my mother had taught me when I was young. According to TCM, cold food and drinks can damage the spleen, not only the organ itself but also the entire system of the 'earth' element in the body. The cold food 'muddies' the earth element, and a surfeit disrupts the efficient functioning of the spleen, which serves to absorb nutrients. This could, in turn, affect the entire immune system.

Traditional Chinese medicine has been part of everyday life in East Asia for thousands of years. I was so curious about the theories behind TCM and its mysterious practices that I took an evening class on acupuncture (針灸; $zhen^1$ jiu^3) when I was studying for my first Master's degree in Taipei. My teacher was a well-respected professor in both Taiwan and China. I thought the course would be mainly theoretical, but she made all students start practising on themselves just 10 minutes into the first lesson. I picked up a long, thin, sterilized needle and poked it into my HeGu (合谷), located between the thumb and forefinger. I felt pain and an electrical shock across my left arm. I wasn't sure I was doing it right, but simply tried to follow the instructions. That same evening, we stuck needles into several other points on the legs, feet and elbows. I continued my weekly course and practised diligently. I was so much into my acupuncture that my parents or room-mates often discovered me in the morning with needles in my face and limbs because I had fallen asleep before I remembered to 'unplug' them.

A few years ago my sister Anchi came to London. She was suffering from tennis elbow. I took her to hospital for an operation and was amazed to see that the 'Western' procedure (arthroscopy) performed by the doctor bore some resemblance to acupuncture. Sceptics often argue that TCM has no scientific basis. It's not up to me to judge. All I know is, years after the intensive training and practice, my acupuncture skills are very rusty. Yet I greatly value the knowledge I gained. I learned how to take a more holistic view of the human body and how to be mindful of every sensation we experience. My studies also taught me to be humble: there is far more we don't know than we already know.

CHAPTER 8

TRAVEL

車 car (che[1])

This character represents a wooden cart and means 'vehicle'. In ancient China, carts were mainly used as part of the battle force during war; the more carts you had, the stronger your army. Gradually, carts of this type came to be used for transporting goods and people, too.

A more common definition for 車 is 'car'. Sometimes the phrase 車子 (che[1] zi) is used instead. While the character 車 can be used on its own, the addition of the suffix 子 (see p. 72) emphasizes that you are referring to the modern type of vehicle. The simplified form of the character is 车.

舟 boat (zhou[1])

This character depicts the shape of an ancient Chinese wooden vessel, which looked similar to a punt. 舟 is quite an archaic way of expressing 'boat'. Today we tend to use the compound character 船 (chuan[2]), which is a combination of 舟, 'how many'/'small table' 几 (see p. 160) and 'mouth' 口.

If you see 舟 in a compound character, you know it means something to do with boats or ships. For example, 'sampan' 舢 (shan[1]) – a flat-bottomed wooden boat – is a combination of 'boat' 舟 and 'mountain' 山. 'Kayak' 舠 (dao[1]) is a combination of 'boat' 舟 and 'knife' 刀 (see p. 192). This is a rare character, however, mainly because modern kayaking is not part of Chinese tradition.

火車 train

(huo³ che¹)

fire + vehicle = train

Trains were originally powered by steam and fire, so that's why 'fire' 火 plus 'vehicle' 車 means 'train'.

公車 bus

(gong¹ che¹)

public + vehicle = bus

The characters 'public' 公 (gong¹) and 'vehicle' 車 together mean 'bus'. Another common way to express 'bus' is 公交車 (gong¹ jiao¹ che¹). 交 (jiao¹) means 'to exchange', 'to intersect' or 'to make' (as in 'to make friends'; see p. 188).

汽車 car/automobile

(qi⁴ che¹)

steam + vehicle = car/automobile

This phrase usually refers to saloon cars.

小汽車 compact car (xiao³ qi⁴ che¹)

small + steam + car/automobile = compact car

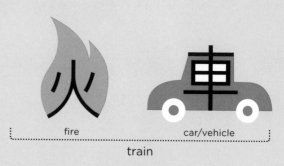

fire　　　car/vehicle

train

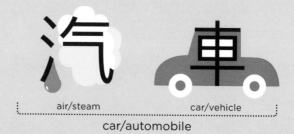

public　　　car/vehicle

bus

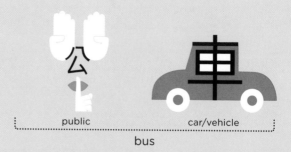

air/steam　　　car/vehicle

car/automobile

small　　　air/steam　　　car/vehicle

compact car

horse   car/vehicle

horse-drawn carriage

cow/ox   car/vehicle

ox-drawn cart

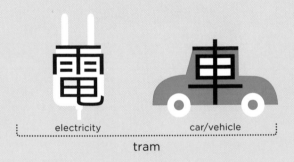

electricity   car/vehicle

tram

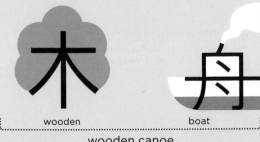

wooden   boat

wooden canoe

馬車 horse-drawn carriage (ma³ che¹)

horse + vehicle = horse-drawn carriage

牛車 ox-drawn cart (niu² che¹)

cow + vehicle = ox-drawn cart

電車 tram (dian⁴ che¹)

electricity + vehicle = tram

Electric cars are becoming increasingly popular these days, but actually the earliest form of transport powered by electricity was the tram; that's why 'electricity' 電 plus 'vehicle' 車 means 'tram'. The longer phrase 電動汽車 (dian⁴ dong⁴ qi⁴ che¹), which translates literally as 'electricity move automobile', is used to refer to 'electric car'.

木舟 wooden canoe (mu⁴ zhou¹)

wooden + boat = wooden canoe

站 to stand/station
(zhan⁴)

This character is phono-semantic (or pictophonetic): 'to stand' 立 (li⁴) indicates the meaning, while 'to occupy' 占 (zhan⁴) indicates the pronunciation. When it is used as a noun, the character commonly means 'stand' or 'station'.

开 to open/ to drive (kai[1])

This is the simplified form of the character; the traditional form is 開, which is a combination of 'door' 門 (men[2]) and 开, which is useful to memorize as a pair of hands opening the bolt on a door.

In addition to its main meaning, 'to open', this character is used in reference to making something begin or start. For example, we make appliances start to function; we 'turn on' something. We make a stationary vehicle start moving; we 'drive'. Thus, this character commonly means 'to turn on' or 'to drive'.

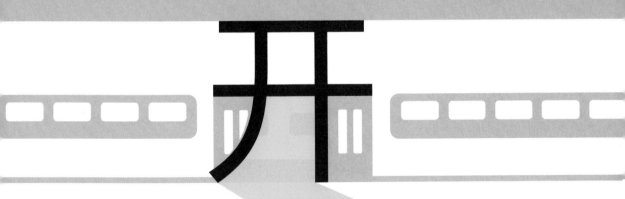

几 how many (ji³)

Don't you think this building block looks similar to the symbol for pi (π)? Interestingly, its meaning has something to do with maths, too; it means 'how many'. This is the simplified form of the character; the traditional form is 幾.

几 is a very useful question-word. For example, 几天? (ji³ tian¹?) means 'how many days?' and 几点? (ji³ dian³?), which translates literally as 'how many o'clock?', means 'what time?'

When 几 is pronounced as 'ji¹', it means 'small table'.

....

机 machine (ji¹)

This character is a combination of 'tree' 木 and 'how many' 几. You can imagine a giant machine eating up all the trees. What a nightmare! This is the simplified form of the character; the traditional form is 機.

飞 to fly (fei[1])

Originally, this character depicted a bird flapping its wings and flying upwards. Its meaning has been extended to indicate 'to fly'. When it is used as an adjective it means 'flying'. This is the simplified form of the character; the traditional form is 飛.

When we add 飞 and 船 together, we have 'flying boat' 飞船 (fei[1] chuan[2]).

上車 to get in a car (shang[4] che[1])

to ascend + car/vehicle = to get in a car

This phrase also refers to getting in or on most road vehicles, as well as on a train.

坐車 to travel by car (zuo[4] che[1])

to sit + car/vehicle = to travel by car

When you 'sit' 坐 (zuo[4]) in or on a vehicle, you travel by it. As well as 'to travel by car', this phrase can be applied to travelling by train, bus or taxi.

下車 to get out of a car (xia[4] che[1])

to descend + car/vehicle = to get out of a car

As in the case of the phrase 上車, this phrase can be applied to any form of road vehicle, as well as a train.

飞机 plane (fei[1] ji[1])

flying + machine = plane

What comes to your mind when you think of a 'flying machine'? An aeroplane, of course!

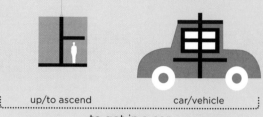

up/to ascend · car/vehicle

to get in a car

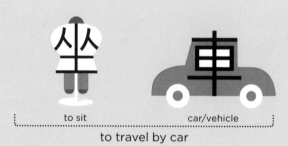

to sit · car/vehicle

to travel by car

down/to descend · car/vehicle

to get out of a car

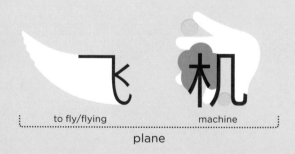

to fly/flying · machine

plane

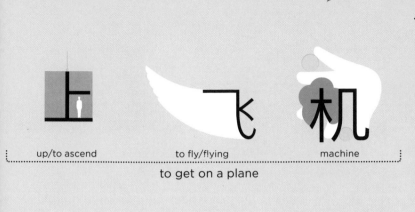

up/to ascend · to fly/flying · machine

to get on a plane

to drive · to fly/flying · machine

fly a plane

to sit · to fly/flying · machine

to travel by plane

down/to descend · to fly/flying · machine

to get off a plane

上飞机 to get on a plane (shang⁴ fei¹ ji¹)

to ascend + plane = to get on a plane

The short form of this phrase is 上机 (shang⁴ ji¹).

开飞机 to fly a plane (kai¹ fei¹ ji¹)

to drive + plane = to fly a plane

The phrase 开机 (kai¹ ji¹) doesn't also mean 'to fly a plane'. It actually means 'to turn on a machine'/'to turn on a computer'; 机 is also a common term for 'computer'.

坐飞机 to travel by plane (zuo⁴ fei¹ ji¹)

to sit + plane = to travel by plane

Don't let your imagination get carried away: 坐机 doesn't actually mean anything!

下飞机 to get off a plane (xia⁴ fei¹ ji¹)

to descend + plane = to get off a plane

The short form of this phrase is 下机 (xia⁴ ji¹).

火車站
train station
(huo³ che¹ zhan⁴)

train + station

火車 means 'train' and
站 means 'station', so
火車站 is 'train station'
– easy!

公車站
bus station
(gong¹ che¹ zhan⁴)

bus + station

公車 means 'bus' and
站 means 'station', so
公車站 is 'bus station'.

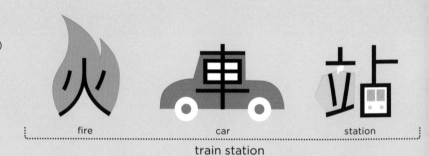

fire   car   station

train station

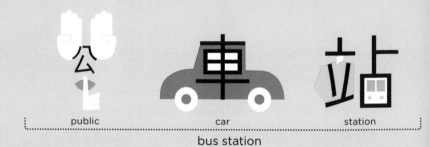

public   car   station

bus station

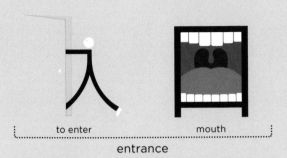

to enter   mouth

entrance

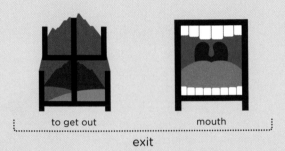

to get out   mouth

exit

to get out   to enter   mouth

gateway

入口 entrance
(ru⁴ kou³)

to enter + mouth = entrance

This simple phrase contains the building blocks 'to enter' 入 (ru⁴) and 'mouth' 口. In this context, 口 means 'entrance', just like the mouth is an entrance into the body, and the character 入 refers to the act of entering. Literally, this phrase expresses 'entering through the entrance'.

出口 exit
(chu¹ kou³)

to get out + mouth = exit

A 'mouth' 口 that tells you where 'to get out' 出 (chu¹) means 'exit'.

出入口 gateway
(chu¹ ru⁴ kou³)

to get out + to enter + mouth = gateway

Something that allows you either 'to get out' of or 'to enter' a space is a 'gateway'.

Let's explore further

China's economic growth and the motor industry

In 1999, as an internet whizz-kid with my own start-up company, I made several trips to Beijing and Shanghai. At that time both cities were massive building sites. I enjoyed my adventures, hopping around between run-down brick buildings and giant construction sites. Both cities were swamped with millions of bicycles and motorbikes. I was wide-eyed with amazement at the impressive barrel-vaulted atrium of the Hyatt hotel at the top of the Jin Mao Tower in the Pudong district of Shanghai. After a super-expensive drink with some friends, I left that golden, shiny building thinking that China's burgeoning economic growth was going to take over the world. I waited for a taxi at the entrance to the hotel, but none came. What I noticed instead was a whirlpool of yellow dust – a coming sandstorm. I waited for ten minutes and then gave up. In fact, taxis did not operate in Pudong at that time, so I had to find my own way back to my hotel in the Ruijin area. The street in front of the Hyatt was still under construction, and all I could see was yellow sand in the murky sky. Several hundred metres further on, I spotted a few motorbikes and scooters parked among some street-food stalls. I found my taxi. I paid the driver 5 yuan, and he asked me to get on the back of his rickety motorbike. Twenty minutes later, I arrived back at my hotel with a very sandy face.

I returned to the Jin Mao Tower in 2014 with my children. This time, however, the beautiful building appeared rather modest and unimpressive in comparison with its incredible new neighbours. There were Rolls-Royces, Bentleys and Lamborghinis queuing outside the skyscrapers and other landmark buildings.

China's rapid economic growth is probably best exemplified by the motor industry. In 2009 China overtook the United States to become the biggest automotive market in the world. And from 2005 until 2030, China is set to witness tenfold growth in its car market. However, China's roads have the highest death rates worldwide: in 2005 the World Health Organization reported that every day about 45,000 people were injured and 680 killed in road accidents. According to statistics dating from 2012, China is home to only 3 percent of the world's vehicles, but accounts for 24 percent of traffic fatalities worldwide.

In Shanghai I hired a friendly driver called Wang to take us to West Lake (西湖; xi[1] hu[2]). He seemed to enjoy chatting to us about his dreams of sending his children to the United States for their higher education. He was envious of his friends who managed to send their children abroad early enough to acquire smart English accents. I looked into his eyes and saw a man with dreams. I suddenly realized that, behind the economic growth and the dizzying rate of construction, behind any statistics presented to us, lies something much more basic and fundamental that drives us: it's love – love for our children and our families, and our commitment to provide them with a better life. In Wang's mind, sending his children to America – a country he'd never visited – would guarantee their education and their whole future.

CHAPTER 9

CITIES & COUNTRIES

東 east (dong¹)

When we see the 'sun' 日 coming up between the 'trees' 木, we know we're looking 'east' 東. The simplified form of the character is 东.

西 west (xi¹)

In oracle-bone script, this character represented a nest. In seal script, a bird was added next to it, to indicate that birds retire to their nests. Later the character came to mean 'west', since after a day spent flying around, tired birds head home when the sun sets in the west. I see a cowboy in the Wild West in this character.

南 south (nan²)

Originally, this character was a pictograph of a percussion instrument. This meaning has been lost for a long time, and now the character means only 'south'. To me, a strong association with the south are penguins in Antarctica.

北 north (bei³)

In oracle-bone script, this character depicted two people standing back to back, and it meant 'back'; it has now evolved to mean 'north'. I like to imagine that these two people, with their backs to each other, are out in the cold north wind. After scratching my head, wondering how to express 'north' visually, I think that this idea is perfect!

Note that, when mentioned together in Chinese, the cardinal directions always appear in the order 東西南北.

東西 thing/stuff (dong¹ xi)

east + west = thing/stuff

I love this phrase! If we place 'east' 東 and 'west' 西 together, we create 'thing' or 'stuff' 東西. There are several possible explanations for this phrase. One I particularly like is that, between the time the sun rises in the east and sets in the west, it shines on lots of things on Earth.

京 capital (jing[1])

What's the place where all the tall buildings and prominent government officials are situated? It's the capital. 京 is the character for 'capital', and originally it depicted a grand building sited on high ground.

In ancient China, only the ruling class had the privilege of building their palaces or mansions on high ground for strategic, political or military purposes. Over time, the meaning of this character changed from 'a grand building lived in by kings' to 'capital', since the capital city is where the homes of all those political leaders are.

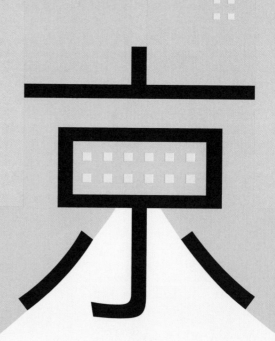

海 sea (hai³)

This character is a combination of the compound form of 'water' 氵 and 'every' 每 (mei³). You can also see 'mother' 母 in it. Every drop of water in our rivers and streams eventually makes its way to the sea, just as children return to their mothers.

A combination of 'water' 氵 and 'sheep' 羊 means 'ocean' 洋 (yang²). The compound 洋 also means 'foreign'; someone or something that crosses an ocean must be 'foreign'. A 'foreign' 洋 'person' 人 is a 'foreigner' 洋人 (yang² ren²).

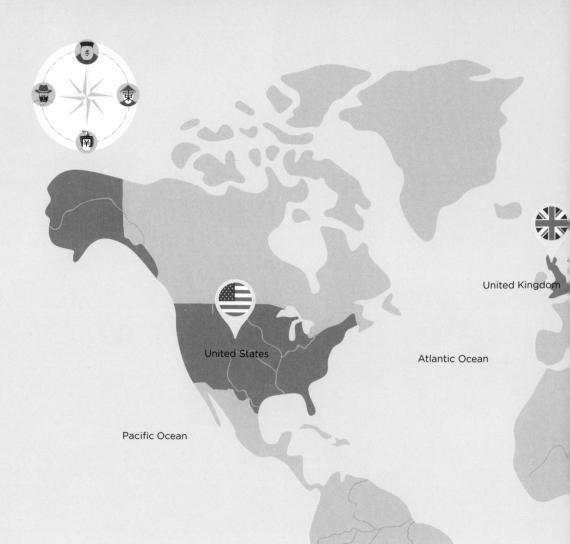

United Kingdom

United States

Atlantic Ocean

Pacific Ocean

中国 China (zhong¹ guo²)

middle + country = China

Historically, 中国 (literally, 'middle nations') referred to the states on the Central Plain. The phrase was used in pre-imperial times to distinguish the people of those states from 'barbarians'; it was not used as the country name until the 19th century. The 'people' 人 from 'China' 中国 are 'Chinese' 中国人 (zhong¹ guo² ren²).

This is the simplified form of the phrase; the traditional form is 中國.

英国 England (ying¹ guo²)

brave + country = England

The character 英 (ying¹) is used as the abbreviation of 'England' because its pronunciation is similar to that of the first syllable in 'England'. The meaning of 英 is 'brave', so 'England' 英国 is a 'brave country'!

美国 United States (mei³ guo²)

beautiful + country = United States

The character 美 (mei³) is used because its pronunciation is similar to that of the second syllable in 'America', and it has a nice meaning: 'beautiful'.

China

Japan

East
China Sea

Pacific Ocean

South
China Sea

日本 Japan (ri⁴ ben³)

sun + origin = Japan

Japan, the 'Land of the Rising Sun', lies east of China,
so when the sun rises, it comes from Japan: 'sun' 日
and 'origin' 本 (ben³) together mean 'Japan'. The
ancient Chinese often referred to the Japanese as
'east ocean/foreign people' 東洋人 (dong¹ yang² ren²),
and to Europeans as 'west ocean/foreign people'
西洋人 (xi¹ yang² ren²).

大西洋 Atlantic Ocean (da⁴ xi¹ yang²;
big + west + ocean)

太平洋 Pacific Ocean (tai⁴ ping² yang²;
extremely + flat + ocean)

北海 North Sea (bei³ hai³; north + sea)

南海 South China Sea (nan² hai³; south + sea)

東海 East China Sea (dong¹ hai³; east + sea)

北美 North America (bei³ mei³; north + beautiful)

南美 South America (nan² mei³; south + beautiful)

方 direction (fang¹)

This character originally depicted the handle of a sword. Its meaning has been extended to signify 'direction', 'square' or 'region'.

東方 east (dong¹ fang¹; east + direction)

西方 west (xi¹ fang¹; west + direction)

南方 south (nan² fang¹; south + direction)

北方 north (bei³ fang¹; north + direction)

These phrases are used specifically in the sense of 'an easterly direction', 'a southerly direction', etc.

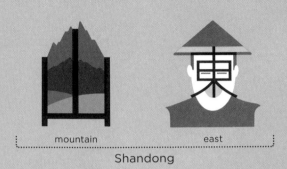

mountain   east

Shandong

four   river

Sichuan

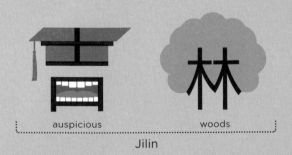

auspicious   woods

Jilin

山東 Shandong
(shan¹ dong¹)

mountain + east = Shandong

The province of Shandong takes its name from its location, east of the Taihang Mountains (太行山; tai⁴ hang² shan¹). It has a population of 97 million.

四川 Sichuan
(si⁴ chuan¹)

four + river = Sichuan

There are various theories about the name 四川: it can refer to 'four' 四 main 'rivers' 川, but it can also mean where 'four plains' meet (in addition to 'river', 川 means 'plain'). The population of the province is 82 million.

吉林 Jilin (ji² lin²)

auspicious + woods = Jilin

The name 'Jilin' originates from Manchu, which was one of the official languages of the Qing dynasty (1644–1912) and remained in fairly wide use until the early 20th century. Jilin in Manchu means 'city by the river', but 吉林 can refer to either the city or the province of the same name. You can add 'province' 省 (sheng³) to the end of the phrase. The population of the province is 27.5 million.

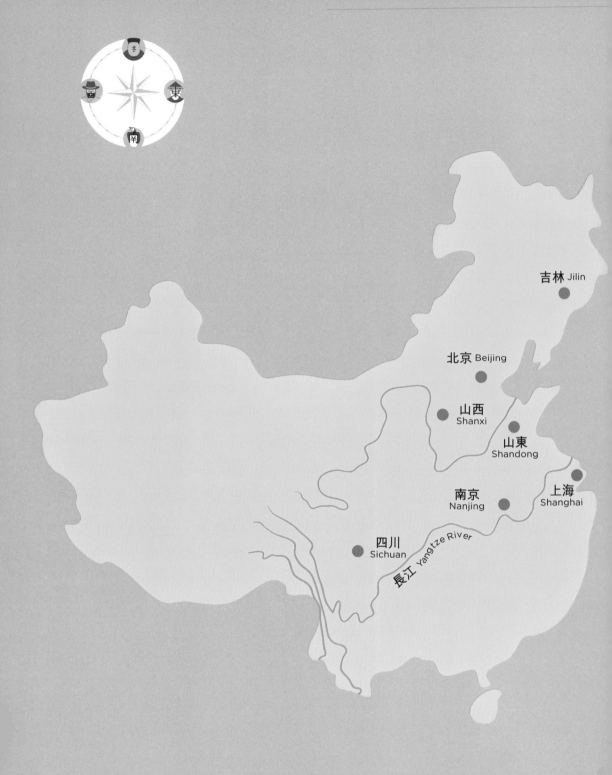

吉林 Jilin

北京 Beijing

山西 Shanxi

山東 Shandong

南京 Nanjing

上海 Shanghai

四川 Sichuan

長江 Yangtze River

北京 Beijing (bei³ jing¹)

north + capital = Beijing

Beijing is the capital city of China, and it has played a major role, both politically and culturally, throughout the history of the country. The city has been known by several different names, including Youzhou, Zhongdu, Dadu, Shuntian, Peiping and Yanjing.

Beijing means 'north/northern capital'. This name was first used during the Ming dynasty (1368-1644), but it became widely accepted only in 1949, at the founding of the People's Republic of China. Whether you call it in English 'Beijing' or 'Peking' (an older English spelling), in Chinese the city is 北京.

南京 Nanjing (nan² jing¹)

south + capital = Nanjing

Nanjing served as the capital city for several Chinese dynasties. At that time, it was regarded as a more historic and central capital than Beijing. As in the case of Beijing, Nanjing has been known by various names throughout history, but the most widely known one is still 南京 – the 'south/southern capital'.

Where is the 'east capital' 東京 (dong¹ jing¹)? It's Tokyo. It was named by the Japanese, not the Chinese, so there is nothing to suggest Chinese colonialism!

上海 Shanghai (shang⁴ hai³)

above + sea = Shanghai

Shanghai – meaning 'above the sea' – is the biggest and busiest city in China. It began as a small agricultural village and developed only during the late Qing dynasty (1644-1912). Since that time it has become the most populous city in the world, with over 24 million inhabitants – that's more people than live in the whole of Taiwan!

長江 Yangtze River (chang² jiang¹)

long + river = Yangtze River

The compound character 江 (jiang¹) is another common way to express 'river'. At 6,300 km (3,900 miles) in length, the Yangtze is the longest river in China, and that's how it got its name, 'long river' 長江.

吉林省 Jilin Province (ji² lin² sheng³)

山西省 Shanxi Province (shan¹ xi¹ sheng³)

山東省 Shandong Province (shan¹ dong¹ sheng³)

四川省 Sichuan Province (si⁴ chuan¹ sheng³)

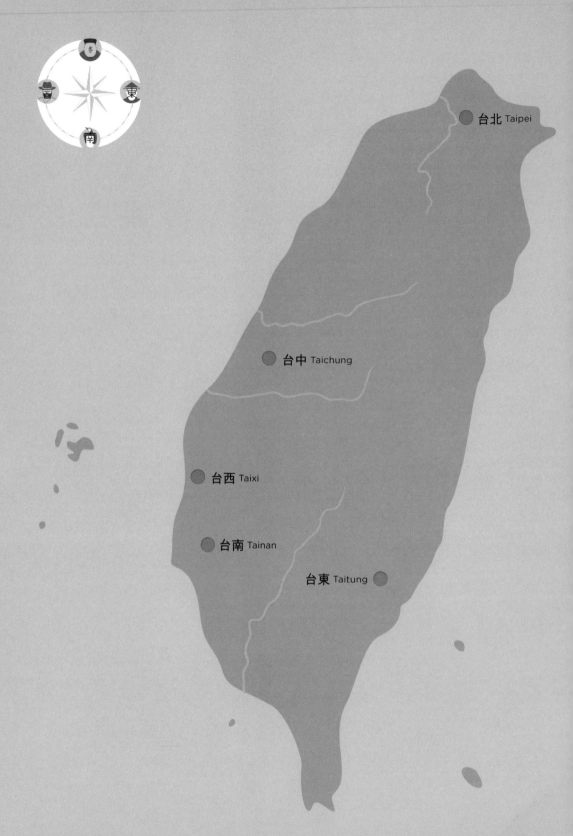

台北 Taipei

台中 Taichung

台西 Taixi

台南 Tainan

台東 Taitung

台北 Taipei (tai² bei³)

Taiwan + north = Taipei

The character 台 (tai²) is a combination of 'private' 厶 (si¹) and 口 'mouth', and means 'platform'. It's also commonly used as an abbreviation of 'Taiwan' 台灣 (tai² wan¹).

Taipei means 'Taiwan north' – the north of Taiwan. As the capital of Taiwan, Taipei City (台北市; tai² bei³ shi⁴ – the official name) is probably also the world capital of food. In June 2015, CNN reported that Taipei is the no. 1 global destination for good food. I grew up there and I'm a fanatical foodie, so I know this is true!

If you go to Taipei, you should visit Yangmingshan (陽明山; yang² ming² shan¹) National Park, on the city outskirts, with its amazing variety of flora and fauna. Yangmingshan is also famous for its hot springs.

台中 Taichung (tai² zhong¹)

Taiwan + middle = Taichung

Taichung is located fairly centrally in Taiwan. It's the third largest city on the island, after Taipei and Kaohsiung (高雄; gao¹ xiong²). Its official name is Taichung City 台中市 (tai² zhong¹ shi⁴).

台南 Tainan (tai² nan²)

Taiwan + south = Tainan

You've probably already worked out that Tainan is in southern Taiwan. It's the island's oldest city and served as the capital until 1894. Tainan is well known for its cultural heritage and gourmet food.

台東 Taitung (tai² dong¹)

Taiwan + east = Taitung

Taitung is situated on the southeastern edge of Taiwan. It's famous for its stunning coastline and wooded landscape, which attract nature lovers the world over.

台西 Taixi (tai² xi¹)

Taiwan + west = Taixi

Taixi is a small town on the west coast of Taiwan. It's renowned for its oyster-farming industry.

Let's explore further

The Taipei MRT map

When you visit any capital city, what map do you usually try to get hold of first? For me, it would be a map of the underground/subway system. My hometown, Taipei – the capital city of Taiwan – has an excellent underground network, which is commonly known as the Taipei MRT (Metropolitan Rapid Transport). The Taipei MRT is modern, clean, efficient and inexpensive to use.

On the Taipei MRT map, each station name is written in both Chinese and English. However, I think it would be fun to apply the knowledge you have learned so far in order to read the station names in Chinese.

Below are some of the station names that include characters taught in this book; the relevant page references appear after the pinyin. If the phrase for a station name includes a character that is not taught in the book, this character is marked with an asterisk.

東門 Dongmen (dong[1] men[2])
- see pp. 170, 144

士林 Shilin (shi[4] lin[2])
- see pp. 79, 49

淡*水 Tamsui (dan[4] shui[3])
- see p. 46

小南門 Xiaonanmen (xiao[3] nan[2] men[2])
- see pp. 120, 170, 144

西門 Ximen (xi[1] men[2])
- see pp. 170, 144

北門 Beimen (bei[3] men[2])
- see pp. 170, 144

中山 Zhongshan (zhong[1] shan[1])
- see pp. 128, 88

松*山 Songshan (song[1] shan[1])
- see p. 88

海山 Haishan (hai[3] shan[1])
- see pp. 173, 88

大安* Daan (da[4] an[1])
- see p. 63

象山 Xiangshan (xiang[4] shan[1])
- see pp. 113, 88

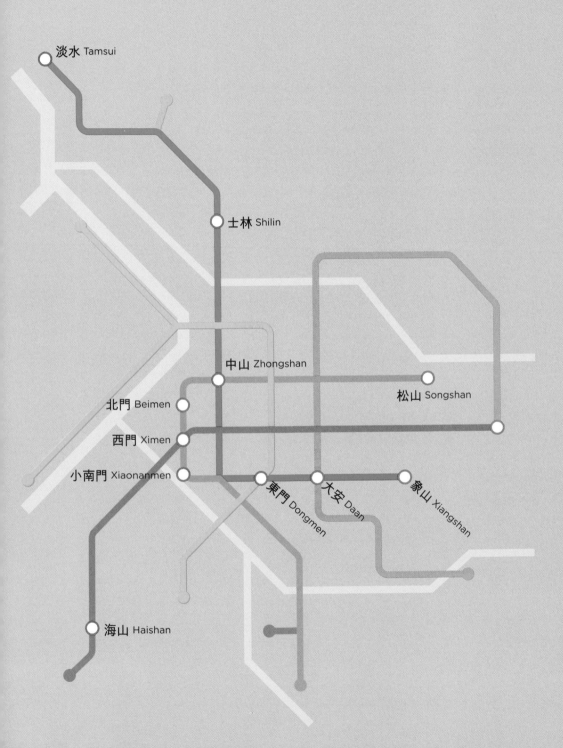

淡水 Tamsui

士林 Shilin

中山 Zhongshan

松山 Songshan

北門 Beimen

西門 Ximen

小南門 Xiaonanmen

東門 Dongmen

大安 Daan

象山 Xiangshan

海山 Haishan

CHAPTER 10

MODERN LIFE

网 net (wang³)

This is the simplified form of the character for 'net'; the traditional form is 網, which is a combination of 'silk' 糸 (mi⁴) and 'to deceive' 罔 (wang³). The simplified version is actually closer to the original pictograph, so let's stick with that. 网 can refer to a physical object or, just as in English, it can serve as the abbreviation of 'internet'.

⺲ is the form of the character used as a component in certain compounds.

上网 to surf the internet (shang⁴ wang³)

to go up + net = to surf the internet

下网 (xia⁴ wang³)

to get off + net

Depending on the context, this phrase means either 'to get off the net [internet]' or 'to put down the [physical] net'.

友 friend (you³)

In oracle-bone inscriptions, this character depicted two right hands drawn together, in reference to two people shaking hands and becoming friends.

Two 'moons' together, 朋 (peng²), also means 'friend' or 'companion'. 朋 represents two people hanging out together, keeping each other company. 友 represents two hands stuck together, implying that they support and help each other.

In modern Chinese, 朋 and 友 share the same meaning. However, 友 is much more common; 朋 is rarely used, except in phrases or idioms. Add 朋 and 友 together, it still means 'friend': 朋友 (peng² you³).

好朋友 (hao³ peng² you³) means 'good friend'. Sometimes we abbreviate this as 好友 (hao³ you³), but we never say 好朋.

豬朋狗友 (zhu¹ peng² gou³ you³; literally, 'pig friend dog dude') is a common idiom describing friends who are a bad influence.

网友 online friend (wang³ you³)

net + friend = online friend

This phrase is a convention, so don't say 网朋友 or 网朋. People will roll their eyes if you get it wrong!

男朋友 boyfriend
(nan² peng² you³)

male + friend = boyfriend

Instead of meaning 'male friend', the phrase 男朋友 refers to a male friend who you are seeing or dating. It is often abbreviated as 男友 (nan² you³).

女朋友 girlfriend
(nü³ peng² you³)

female + friend = girlfriend

Instead of meaning 'female friend', the phrase 女朋友 refers to a female friend who you are seeing or dating. It can also be expressed as 女友 (nü³ you³).

So how do we say 'to get a girlfriend (or boyfriend)'? We use the verb 'to exchange'/ 'to submit' 交 (jiao¹). 'To get a girlfriend' is 交女朋友 (jiao¹ nü³ peng² you³). 交 also means 'to make', as in 'to make friends' 交朋友 (jiao¹ peng² you³).

小朋友 children
(xiao³ peng² you³)

small + friend = children

male   friend

boyfriend

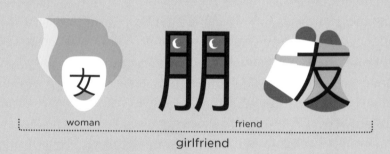

woman   friend

girlfriend

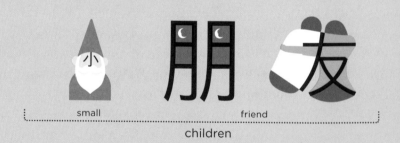

small   friend

children

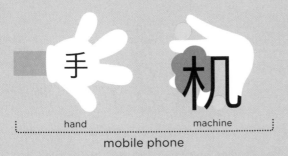

hand · machine

mobile phone

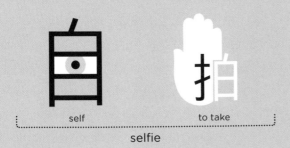

self · to take

selfie

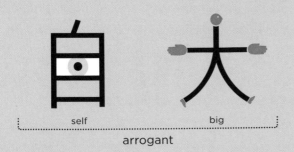

self · big

arrogant

手机 mobile/cell phone (shou³ ji¹)

hand + machine = mobile/cell phone

This phrase is both cool and intuitive! In modern life, what do we hold in our hands most of the time? Clue: it's not a baguette, nor a rose. It's a mobile phone!

自拍 selfie (zi⁴ pai¹)

self + to take = selfie

In 1839 the American Robert Cornelius took what may have been the first photographic self-portrait – the first selfie! 自 means 'self' (see p. 141) and 拍 (pai¹) means 'to take (a picture)'. In the past few years, 自拍 has become a global activity; billions of people do it on a daily basis. 自拍 can be used as a noun or a verb, depending on the context.

自大 arrogant (zi⁴ da⁴)

self + big = arrogant

When someone is full of himself (自), thinking that he's the biggest (大) guy in the world, he has a big ego and is 'arrogant'.

球 ball (qiu²)

This character is a combination of 王, the alternative form of 'jade' 玉 (yu⁴), which indicates the meaning, and 'to demand' 求 (qiu²), which indicates the pronunciation.

Originally, the character referred to a round-shaped jade (王) that was in excessive demand (求). It has since evolved to mean 'ball'. When used as an adjective, the character means 'round' or 'spherical'.

In Chinese, we 'hit' 打 (da³) the ball to express 'to play the ball game'. The literal meaning of 打 is 'to hit', but in this context it means 'to play', as in 'to play golf' or 'to play tennis'.

The friends with whom you play ball are your 球友 (qiu² you³; literally, 'ball friends'). However, when Roger Federer and Novak Djokovic compete at Wimbledon, they are not 'tennis buddies' 球友; they are 'competitors' 對手/对手 (dui⁴ shou³). You should recognize the character 'hand' 手 in this phrase. The character 對/对 (dui⁴) means 'to oppose', 'to face' or 'to correct' when used as a verb; when used as a noun, it means 'pair' or 'couple'.

hand + ball

handball

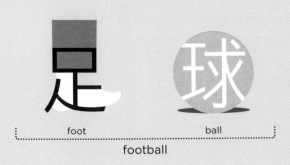

foot + ball

football

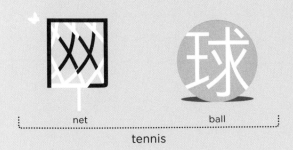

net + ball

tennis

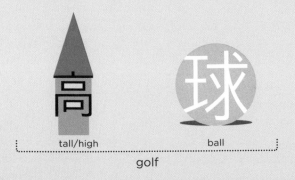

tall/high + ball

golf

手球 handball
(shou³ qiu²)

hand + ball = handball

足球 football
(zu² qiu²)

foot + ball = football

网球 tennis
(wang³ qiu²)

net + ball = tennis

高球 golf
(gao¹ qiu²)

tall/high + ball = golf

高球 is the abbreviation for 'golf'; the full expression is 高爾夫球/高尔夫球 (gao¹ er³ fu¹ qiu²), which partly mirrors the pronunciation of the English word 'golf'. The phrase 高球 is much easier to remember and is commonly used. It literally means 'high ball'.

球 can be used to describe anything ball-shaped. For example, 火球 (huo³ qiu²) is 'fireball' and 水球 (shui³ qiu²), which translates literally as 'water ball', means 'water polo'. Planet Earth is an 'earth ball' 地球 (di⁴ qiu²).

刀 knife (dao¹)

刀 is a primitive pictograph. It can also mean 'sword'. The 'mouth' 口 of a 'knife' 刀 is the 'blade' or 'knife-edge': 刀口 (dao¹ kou³).

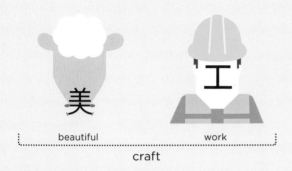

craft

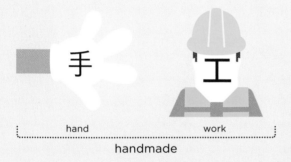

handmade

craft knife

美工 craft
(mei³ gong¹)

beautiful + work = craft

The character 工 is used here as a noun, to refer to a 'piece of work'. When a piece of work is beautifully done, it is a crafted piece.

手工 handmade
(shou³ gong¹)

hand + work = handmade

A piece of work made by hand is 'handmade'.

美工刀 craft knife
(mei³ gong¹ dao¹)

beautiful + work + knife = craft knife

美工 means 'craft' and 刀 means 'knife'. So 美工 + 刀 = 'craft knife' or 'art knife'. The same phrase also refers to a 'box cutter' or 'utility knife'.

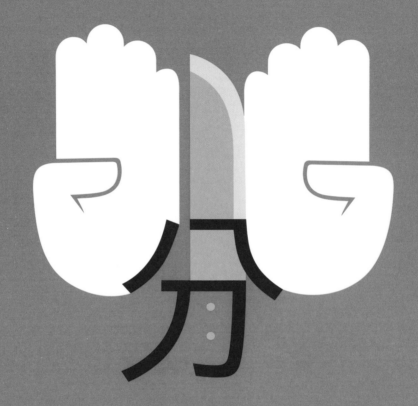

分 to divide (fen¹)

This character is a combination of 'eight' 八 and 'knife' 刀. 八 originally depicted a long stick split in two and meant 'to separate'. Later, 刀 was placed beneath 八 to make the character 分, which represents the act of cutting something in two with a knife and means 'to divide', 'to allocate' or 'to distribute'. When used as a noun, 分 means 'fraction', 'minute' or 'score'.

分手 to break up/to split up (fen¹ shou³)

to divide + hand = to break up/to split up

When two people decide to go their own ways, they break up and don't hold hands (手) any more.

分心 to be distracted (fen¹ xin¹)

to divide + heart = to be distracted

When you 'divide' 分 your 'heart' 心, you're distracted.

分开/分開 to separate/to be apart (fen¹ kai¹)

to divide + to open = to separate/to be apart

The character 开 ('to open') here doesn't carry its original meaning; it acts more like a suffix. 分开 is used to describe two objects moving away from each other, and is more widely used than 分手 (although both are used in reference to personal relationships).

力 power/force (li[4])

This character originally meant 'plough'. Ploughs needed strong animals to pull them, so the meaning of 力 was extended to indicate 'power' or 'force'.

功 achievement (gong[1])

A combination of 'work' 工 and 'power' 力, 功 means 'achievement' or 'merit' when used as a noun.

功力 skill (gong[1] li[4])

achievement + power = skill

Achievement and power are often a reflection of skill.

功夫 kung fu (gong[1] fu[1])

achievement + man = kung fu

I like to remember this phrase by thinking that, in the old days, the 'achievements' 功 of a 'man' 夫 depended on his skill at the martial art 'kung fu' 功夫. When used as an adjective, the phrase means 'skilful'.

工夫 effort (gong[1] fu[1])

work + man = effort

This phrase refers to the time and effort spent doing something. Although it has the same pronunciation, 工夫 has a different meaning from 功夫.

言 to say/to speak (yan²)

Although this character looks like a compound, it's actually a building block. In ancient Chinese writings, it closely resembled the character for 'tongue' 舌 (see p. 145).

The compound 語 (yu³) means 'language'. This character is a combination of 'to say' 言, 'five' 五 and 'mouth' 口. If we stack 'five' on top of 'mouth', we build 'I'/'my' 吾 (wu²). The simplified form of 語 is 语. Here, the character 言 has turned into its simplified compound form, 讠. However, when it appears on its own, 言 stays the same for both traditional and simplified forms.

話 to talk (hua⁴)

This character is a combination of 'to say' 言 and 'tongue' 舌. It means 'to talk', or 'talk' when used as a noun. The simplified form is 话. Note the use of the simplified compound form of 言, 讠, here. However, in modern Chinese the verb 'to talk' is more commonly expressed as the phrase 說話 (shuo¹ hua⁴; simplified form: 说话).

電話 telephone (dian⁴ hua⁴)

electricity + to talk = telephone

What piece of electrical equipment transmits your speech? A telephone! The simplified form is 电话.

示 to reveal (shi⁴)

This building block is fairly easy to read, but make sure you don't confuse it with such building blocks as 'small' 小 (see p. 120) and 'sky' 天 (see p. 55). It originally depicted a stone table used for making sacrifices to the gods. Make a sacrificial offering and the gods may reveal themselves to you!

礻 is the form of this character used as a component in certain compounds. It's often used in phrases that are related to religion or gods.

視 to observe (shi⁴)

This character is a combination of 礻, the compound form of 'to reveal', which indicates the pronunciation, and 'to see' 見 (jian⁴), which indicates the meaning. It means 'to observe' or 'to look at'. The simplified form is 视.

電視 television (dian⁴ shi⁴)

electricity + to observe = television

Before computers became so popular, what piece of electrical equipment did we spend so much time looking at? It's the television! The simplified form is 电视.

Let's explore further

Basic Chinese grammar

Chinese grammar is easy for a couple of reasons. First, verbs do not take different tenses. In English, we must distinguish between the tenses. For example: I drive a car (present simple); I am driving a car (present continuous); I have driven a car (present perfect); I drove a car (past simple); I will drive a car (future). In Chinese, we just need to say 我開車/我开车 (wo³ kai¹ che¹). To know when I drive a car, we add the time – today/tomorrow/yesterday/one hour ago/right at this moment, etc. – at the start of the sentence.

Secondly, in Chinese there are no strict rules about gender. In spoken Chinese, 'he', 'she' and 'it' are all pronounced as 'ta¹'. In written Chinese, there are gender distinctions: 'he' 他 (with a 'person' building block), 'she' 她 (with a 'woman' building block) and 'it' 它 (with a 'roof' building block). However, many people always use 'he' 他.

Sentence structure in Chinese is also easy. In the table below I have categorized three basic types of sentence.

SENTENCE TYPE	CHINESE	ENGLISH
Type 1: Simple structure SVO (subject + verb + object)	我 想 你。(wo³ xiang³ ni³) [literally] I miss you.	'I miss you.'
Type 2: Add time	In Chinese, time comes at the beginning of a sentence, or right after the subject.	In English, time can come at the beginning or the end of a sentence.
TSVO (time + subject + verb + object) or STVO (subject + time + verb + object)	TSVO: 明天 我 开 飞机。 (ming² tian¹ wo³ kai¹ fei¹ ji¹) [literally] Tomorrow I fly plane. STVO: 我 明天 开 飞机。 (wo³ ming² tian¹ kai¹ fei¹ ji¹) [literally] I tomorrow fly plane	'Tomorrow I will fly a plane,' **or** 'I will fly a plane tomorrow.'
Type 3: Add location	In Chinese, time always comes before location.	In English, time can come before or after location.
STVL (subject + time + verb + location)	他 明天 去 中国。 (ta¹ ming² tian¹ qu⁴ zhong¹ guo²) [literally] He tomorrow go China.	'Tomorrow he is going to China,' **or** 'He is going to China tomorrow.'
STLVO (subject + time + location + verb + object)	小女 天天 在家 上 网。 (xiao³ nü³ tian¹ tian¹ zai⁴ jia¹ shang⁴ wang³) [literally] Small girl every day at home surfs the internet.	'Every day my daughter surfs the internet at home,' **or** 'My daughter surfs the internet at home every day.'

Note: For clarity, spaces have been added between the different grammatical elements in the Chinese sentences.

Modern Chinese words

Just as is the case in English, the Chinese language has adapted to modern life by adopting some loan words (for example, 'golf' 高球), contractions and slang, especially phrases that are related to the widespread use of technology. In this chapter, we have learned, for instance, 'online friend' 网友 and 'selfie' 自拍. Here are some other popular phrases:

ENGLISH	CHINESE	LITERAL TRANSLATION
computer	電腦 (dian⁴ nao³)	electric brain
movie/film	電影 (dian⁴ ying³)	electric shadow
Bluetooth	藍牙 (lan² ya²)	blue tooth
wireless	無線 (wu² xian⁴)	no wire/thread
male geek/nerd	宅男* (zhai² nan²)	house male
female geek/nerd	宅女* (zhai² nü³)	house female

*In Chinese, the phrases 宅男 and 宅女 are used to describe people who spend a lot of time on the computer. They tend to entertain themselves with games, TV and movies. They don't go out much or interact a great deal with people in the real world, and they may lack social skills.

CHAPTER 11

FOOD & DRINK

吃 to eat (chi¹)

This is probably the most important character in Chinese history! When people greet you in China, instead of asking, 'How have you been?', they often enquire, 'Have you eaten?'

The character is a combination of 'mouth' 口 and 'to beg' 乞 (qi³). When your mouth begs, it wants to eat. Before it took on its present meaning, 吃 actually meant 'to stutter'.

大吃 to eat a lot (da⁴ chi¹)

big + to eat = to eat a lot

小吃 street food/snack (xiao³ chi¹)

small + to eat = street food/snack

Street food is part of daily life for most Chinese, and indeed across the whole of Asia: millions of people have their breakfast, lunch and even dinner at street-food stalls every day.

吃東西 to eat something (chi¹ dong¹ xi)

to eat + stuff = to eat something

東西 is 'thing' or 'stuff' (see p. 170), so 'to eat stuff' means 'to eat something'.

喝 to drink (he¹)

This character is a combination of 'mouth' 口, indicating the meaning, and 'a shouting noise' 曷 (he²), indicating the pronunciation. One way to remember the meaning of the character is to think that when we shout loudly, we become very thirsty and so we then need to drink.

喝水 to drink water (he¹ shui³)

to drink + water

大吃大喝 to make a pig of oneself (da⁴ chi¹ da⁴ he¹)

big + to eat + big + to drink = to make a pig of oneself

This common idiom – literally, 'big eat, big drink' – is a reference to eating and drinking a lot, like a pig. But, actually, what's wrong with being a pig? I'm one!

茶 tea (cha[2])

I always imagine this character as a person (人) wandering through a garden of tea trees (木), picking the tips of the tea leaves (艹; see below).

艹 grass (cao[3])

艹 doesn't exist as a stand-alone character; it appears only as part of a compound. Sometimes 艹 is written as 艸, rather like two cacti sitting next to each other. 艸 is the most common building block in the *Kangxi Dictionary*, which was the standard Chinese dictionary in the 18th and 19th centuries.

草 grass (cao[3])

The single character for 'grass' is a combination of 'grass' 艹, indicating the meaning, and 'early morning' 早 (zao[3]), indicating the pronunciation.

苗 bud (miao[2])

Tips of 'grass' 艹 sprouting in a 'field' 田 (tian[2]) make a 'bud' 苗.

苦 bitter (ku[3])

This character is a combination of 'grass' 艹 and 'old' 古 (gu[3]). Old grass must taste rather bitter.

酒 wine (jiu³)

This character is a combination of 'three dots of water' 氵 (the compound form of 'water'; see p. 46) and 'wine vessel' 酉 (see below). The liquid inside a wine vessel is most likely to be wine! 酒 is actually a general noun indicating an alcoholic beverage, such as 'wine', 'spirit' or 'liquor'.

Add 'white' 白 and 'wine' 酒 together, we get 'white spirit' 白酒 (bai² jiu³), a very strong alcoholic drink distilled from sorghum. The same phrase also refers to white wine made from grapes. White spirit used to be very popular in China, but these days more and more people drink 'red wine' 紅酒 (hong² jiu³).

China is the world's largest market for red wine, with 1.86 billion bottles sold in 2013. One reason may be because red is considered lucky in Chinese culture.

In a Chinese restaurant the waiter may ask if you want 酒水 (jiu³ shui³; wine + water). 酒水 refers to both alcoholic and non-alcoholic drinks.

酉 wine vessel (you³)

This character originally took the shape of a jar, and meant 'wine'. The curved strokes still look like the neck of a bottle. Today it's used more specifically to refer to a 'wine vessel'.

米 rice (mi³)

In oracle-bone inscriptions, this character depicted uncooked grains of rice on a wooden rack. In seal inscriptions, the rack became a cross (十), and the rice was indicated by four dots.

米 usually refers to husked, uncooked rice. The character 飯 (fan⁴; simplified form: 饭) means 'cooked rice'. To most Chinese people, a bowl of cooked rice turns any dish into a hearty meal. It's no wonder that China produces and consumes more rice than any other country.

If we 'divide' 分 or grind 'uncooked rice' 米, we turn it into 'powder' 粉 (fen³).

大米 rice (da⁴ mi³)

big + rice = rice

This phrase refers to rice that has been polished and is ready for sale.

小米 millet (xiao³ mi³)

small + rice = millet

Generally, millet grains are smaller than rice grains.

玉米 corn (yu⁴ mi³)

jade + rice = corn

Corn was once rare in China, as precious as jade.

面 noodle (mian⁴)

This is the simplified form of 'noodle'; the traditional form is 麵, which is a combination of 'wheat' 麥 (mai⁴), indicating the meaning, and 'face' 面 (mian⁴), indicating the pronunciation. The simplified form of 'noodle', 面, was chosen as a replacement for the traditional form, 麵, because the characters are pronounced identically.

If we put 'noodle' 面 and 'powder' 粉 together, we make the phrase for 'flour': 面粉 (mian⁴ fen³). This phrase is quite easy to remember because most noodles are made from flour.

果 fruit/nut (guo³)

The original form of this character depicted a fruit-bearing tree. The 'tree' 木 can still be seen in the modern form, but the fruit is now 'field' 田. Imagine that a tree growing in a field bears a lot of fruit: 果.

果 also means 'outcome' or 'result'. Just as is the case in English, when we say that something is 'fruitful', we mean that some achievement has been made.

汁 juice/gravy (zhi¹)

This character is a combination of 'three dots of water' 氵 and 'ten' 十, but here 十 refers to a mixture of many substances.

水果 fruit (shui³ guo³)

water + fruit = fruit

This phrase refers only to 'fruit', whereas 果 can refer to either 'fruit' or 'nut', depending on the context.

果汁 fruit juice (guo³ zhi¹)

fruit + juice

吃水果 to eat fruit (chi¹ shui³ guo³)

to eat + water + fruit = to eat fruit

喝果汁 to drink fruit juice (he¹ guo³ zhi¹)

to drink + fruit + juice

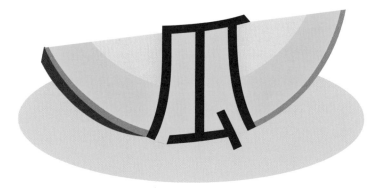

瓜 melon (gua¹)

The earliest form of this character was a pictograph of a large fruit hanging between intertwined vines. The large fruit has now transformed into a shape similar to 'private' 厶 (si¹), but the vines are still well preserved as the curved lines surrounding 厶.

The character 瓜 is often used in reference to any large, fleshy fruit or vegetable with a tough skin; not only 'melon', but also 'gourd', 'squash' and 'calabash'.

魚 fish (yu²)

Today the top part of the character 魚 looks a bit like a fishing hook, but in oracle-bone script it actually resembled the head of a fish. The square sections in the middle of the character used to be angular lines depicting scales, and the strokes at the bottom represented the tail fin. The simplified form of the character is 鱼.

貝 shell (bei⁴)

Cowrie shells were once a popular form of currency in Africa and Asia. For this reason, the character 貝 was often used to refer to 'currency' or 'money'. The simplified form is 贝. When you see 貝 in a compound character, it refers to either something fish-related or something to do with commerce. For example, 'to buy' 買 (mai³; simplified form: 买) is a combination of 'net' 罒 and 'shell' 貝; 'to sell' 賣 (mai⁴; simplified form: 卖) is a combination of 'scholar' 士, 'net' 罒 and 'shell' 貝. 'Wealth' 財 (cai²; simplified form: 财) is a combination of 'shell' 貝 and 'talent' 才 (cai²); 'poor' 貧 (pin²; simplified form: 贫) is a combination of 'to divide' 分 and 'shell' 貝.

蛙 frog (wa¹)

This character is a combination of 'insect' 虫 (chong²), indicating the meaning, and 圭 (gui¹), indicating the pronunciation. In ancient Chinese, the character 圭 was used to represent the rough, low croaking sound that a frog makes.

The phrase 'frog person' 蛙人 (wa¹ ren²) is used to mean 'frogman' or 'diver'. The phrase 'rain frog' 雨蛙 (yu³ wa¹) refers to the genus *Hyla*, belonging to the family of tree frogs. A 'bullfrog' is 牛蛙 (niu² wa¹; cow + frog).

龜 turtle (gui¹)

This character was originally a pictograph of a turtle, with its head, legs and tail sticking out beneath its shell. At the top of the modern form of the character you can see the head, and at the bottom, the tail. The four legs are on the left, and the shell on the right. The character can mean 'tortoise' as well as 'turtle'. The simplified form is 龟 – a similar shape, but with fewer strokes. Oracle-bone inscriptions, the earliest form of Chinese writing, were often inscribed on pieces of turtle shell. It's fitting that some examples have survived because, in Chinese culture, the turtle is associated with long life, wisdom and endurance.

肉 meat (rou⁴)

The original form of this character looked like a thick piece of meat with exposed veins. In its modern form, the veins have been transformed to look like one 'person' 人 standing on top of another, and the component 冂 represents the outline of the meat.

月 is the form of the character used as a component in certain compounds. This modern compound form looks identical to the character for 'moon', 月 (see p. 28). However, in ancient Chinese writing they used to be different: the compound form of 'meat' was written as 月, with unattached diagonal lines across the middle. Over time, 月 has evolved to be written the same way as 'moon' 月.

When you see 'meat' 月 used in a compound character, the meaning is likely to be associated with 'flesh' or related to parts of the body – for example, 'liver' 肝 (gan¹), 'muscle' 肌 (ji¹), 'stomach' 胃 (wei⁴) or 'shoulder' 肩 (jian¹).

The character 肉 is also very useful when we refer to meat, poultry and fish. We build phrases in this simple way: 'animal name' + 'meat'. For example:

beef = cow + meat = 牛肉 (niu² rou⁴)

pork = pig + meat = 豬肉 (zhu¹ rou⁴)

lamb = sheep + meat = 羊肉 (yang² rou⁴)

chicken (poultry) = chicken + meat = 鸡肉 (ji¹ rou⁴)

fish = fish + meat = 魚肉 (yu² rou⁴)

Super-easy!

牛肉面 beef noodle (niu² rou⁴ mian⁴)

cow + meat + noodle = beef noodle

鸡肉面 chicken noodle (ji¹ rou⁴ mian⁴)

chicken + meat + noodle = chicken noodle

肉

鸡

魚

Let's explore further

More food phrases

People often ask me about my favourite Chinese dishes or my favourite Chinese restaurants in a particular city. It's just impossible for me to answer. I grew up in Taipei, where there is no such thing as 'Chinese food'; we differentiate between the cuisines of Shanghai, Beijing, Hunan, Sichuan, Shandong, Guangdong and many other regions. There are regional variations in how food is prepared and cooked, and the choice of ingredients is often dictated by such factors as agricultural abundance, geographic constraints, religion or tradition. My advice is simply to have an open mind. Sometimes we have an unforgettable surprise when we try something new!

山豬 wild boar (shan[1] zhu[1])

mountain + pig = wild boar

牛舌 ox tongue (niu[2] she[2])

cow/ox + tongue = ox tongue

生魚 raw fish (sheng[1] yu[2])

birth/life + fish = raw fish

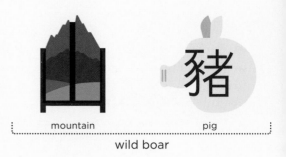

mountain　　　　pig

wild boar

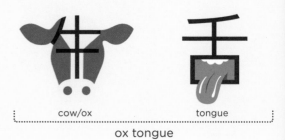

cow/ox　　　　tongue

ox tongue

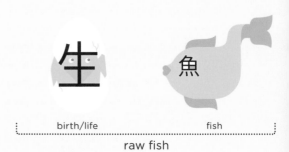

birth/life　　　　fish

raw fish

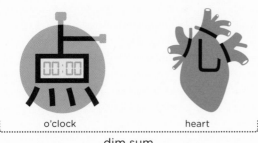

o'clock   heart

dim sum

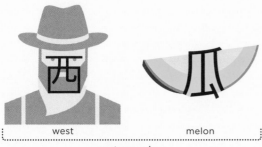

west   melon

watermelon

sheep   meat   noodle

lamb noodle

点心 dim sum
(dian³ xin¹)

点 combined with 心 = a little

a little + heart = dim sum ('a little snack to satisfy your heart')

西瓜 watermelon
(xi¹ gua¹)

west + melon = watermelon

羊肉面 lamb noodle
(yang² rou⁴ mian⁴)

sheep + meat + noodle = lamb noodle

Advanced Phrases & Sentences

Learning Chinese is fun! Once you are able to recognize a few hundred basic characters and phrases, you can start building more complex phrases and even sentences. Here are some examples using characters and phrases you have learned in this book.

An unsettled state of mind (pp. 24, 124, 24, 124)

七上八下

The world is at peace (pp. 55, 124, 63, 130)

天下太平

Life is beautiful (pp. 150, 123, 62, 40)

美好人生

Mobile internet (pp. 146, 160, 124, 186)

手機上網 (traditional Chinese); 手机上网 (simplified Chinese)

Long life; immortality (pp. 132, 40, 122, 125)

長生不老 (traditional Chinese); 长生不老 (simplified Chinese)

The sunrise is beautiful (pp. 28, 150, 123, 150)

日出好美

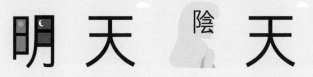

Tomorrow will be cloudy (pp. 30, 55, 56)

明天陰天 (traditional Chinese); 今天阴天 (simplified Chinese)

Westerner (pp. 170, 176, 62)

西方人

Depart from Shanghai (pp. 179, 150, 143)

上海出發 (traditional Chinese); 上海出发 (simplified Chinese)

Fossil-fuel power station (pp. 47, 195, 143, 92, 158)

火力發電站 (traditional Chinese); 火力发电站 (simplified Chinese)

Taipei Railway Station (pp. 181, 156, 158)

台北火車站 (traditional Chinese); 台北火车站 (simplified Chinese)

Spokesperson (pp. 143, 196, 62)

發言人 (traditional Chinese); 发言人 (simplified Chinese)

Locally grown (pp. 48, 40, 132)

土生土長 (traditional Chinese); 土生土长 (simplified Chinese)

Papa is genetically bald (pp. 70, 55, 40, 54, 142)

爸爸天生光頭 (traditional Chinese); 爸爸天生光头 (simplified Chinese)

Mrs Lin doesn't eat meat (pp. 49, 65, 122, 202, 212)

林太太不吃肉

Tennis racket (pp. 191, 150)

網球拍 (traditional Chinese); 网球拍 (simplified Chinese)

America is so huge (pp. 174, 123, 63)

美國好大 (traditional Chinese); 美国好大 (simplified Chinese)

Strong winds and heavy rain (pp. 63, 94, 89)

大風大雨 (traditional Chinese); 大风大雨 (simplified Chinese)

Sichuan giant panda (pp. 177, 63, 104, 110)

四川大熊貓 (traditional Chinese); 四川大熊猫 (simplified Chinese)

天天开心

Be happy every day (pp. 55, 159, 144)

天天開心 (traditional Chinese); 天天开心 (simplified Chinese)

Don't say a word (pp. 22, 196, 122, 143)

一言不發 (traditional Chinese); 一言不发 (simplified Chinese)

Can't tell your left from your right (pp. 126, 127, 122, 194)

左右不分

Confident and natural; blatantly (pp. 63, 176)

大大方方

REFERENCE

Essential Characters

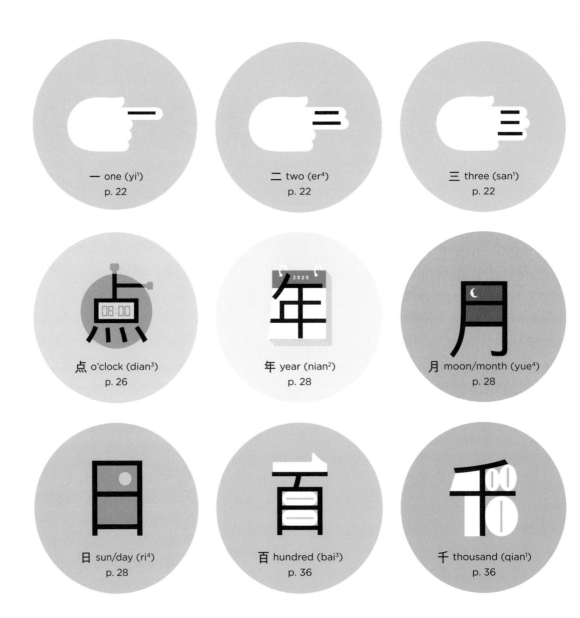

一 one (yi¹)
p. 22

二 two (er⁴)
p. 22

三 three (san¹)
p. 22

点 o'clock (dian³)
p. 26

年 year (nian²)
p. 28

月 moon/month (yue⁴)
p. 28

日 sun/day (ri⁴)
p. 28

百 hundred (bai³)
p. 36

千 thousand (qian¹)
p. 36

元 dollar (yuan²)
p. 37

生 birth (sheng¹)
p. 40

水 water (shui³)
p. 46

火 fire (huo³)
p. 47

土 soil (tu³)
p. 48

木 tree (mu⁴)
p. 49

金 gold (jin¹)
p. 50

星 star (xing¹)
p. 52

光 light (guang¹)
p. 54

天 sky (tian¹)
p. 55

陰 yin (yin¹)
p. 56

陽 yang (yang²)
p. 57

人 person (ren²)
p. 62

众 crowd (zhong⁴)
p. 63

女 woman (nü³)
p. 66

男 man (nan²)
p. 67

父 father (fu⁴)
p. 68

母 mother (mu³)
p. 69

爸 dad (ba⁴)
p. 70

媽 mum (ma¹)
p. 71

子 son/child (zi³)
p. 72

王 king (wang²)
p. 74

主 master (zhu³)
p. 75

工 work (gong¹)
p. 76

巫 witch (wu¹)
p. 77

丑 clown (chou³)
p. 78

士 scholar (shi⁴)
p. 79

佛 Buddha (fo²)
p. 82

后 queen/empress (hou⁴)
p. 85

山 mountain (shan¹)
p. 88

川 river (chuan¹)
p. 88

雨 rain (yu³)
p. 89

气 air (qi⁴)
p. 93

风 wind (feng¹)
p. 94

石 stone (shi²)
p. 95

牛 cow (niu²)
p. 104

熊 bear (xiong[2])
p. 104

馬 horse (ma[3])
p. 105

羊 sheep (yang[2])
p. 105

蛇 snake (she[2])
p. 106

兔 rabbit (tu[4])
p. 106

鸡 chicken (ji[1])
p. 107

鼠 rat (shu[3])
p. 107

犬 dog (quan[3])
p. 108

狗 dog (gou[3])
p. 108

豬 pig (zhu¹)
p. 109

猴 monkey (hou²)
p. 110

鳥 bird (niao³)
p. 111

毛 hair; fur (mao²)
p. 112

象 elephant (xiang⁴)
p. 113

龙 dragon (long²)
p. 116

虎 tiger (hu³)
p. 116

大 big (da⁴)
p. 120

小 small (xiao³)
p. 120

又 again (you⁴)
p. 121

不 not; no (bu⁴)
p. 122

上 up; above (shang⁴)
p. 124

下 down; below (xia⁴)
p. 124

老 old (lao³)
p. 125

左 left (zuo³)
p. 126

右 right (you⁴)
p. 127

中 middle (zhong¹)
p. 128

平 equal (ping²)
p. 130

半 half (ban⁴)
p. 131

長 long; to grow
(chang²) p. 132

高 tall; high (gao¹)
p. 133

口 mouth (kou³)
p. 138

耳 ear (er³)
p. 140

目 eye (mu⁴)
p. 141

头 head (tou²)
p. 142

发 hair (fa³)
p. 143

心 heart (xin¹)
p. 144

舌 tongue (she²)
p. 145

足 foot (zu²)
p. 147

骨 bone (gu³)
p. 148

車 car (che¹)
p. 154

舟 boat (zhou¹)
p. 155

站 stand; station (zhan⁴)
p. 158

几 how many (ji³)
p. 160

飞 fly (fei¹)
p. 161

東 east (dong¹)
p. 170

西 west (xi¹)
p. 170

南 south (nan²)
p. 170

北 north (bei³)
p. 170

京 capital (jing¹)
p. 172

海 sea (hai³)
p. 173

方 direction (fang¹)
p. 176

网 net (wang³)
p. 186

友 friend (you³)
p. 187

球 ball (qiu²)
p. 190

刀 knife (dao¹)
p. 192

吃 to eat (chi¹)
p. 202

喝 to drink (he¹)
p. 203

茶 tea (cha²)
p. 204

酒 wine (jiu³)
p. 205

果 fruit; nut (guo³)
p. 208

魚 fish (yu²)
p. 210

貝 shell (bei⁴)
p. 210

肉 meat (rou⁴)
p. 212

馬

馬

馬 horse
虫 bug
牛 cow
小 small

仙 immortal
魚 fish
飞 fly
戶 household

鳥　火

林 woods
木 tree/wooden
鹿 deer
鳥 bird
羽 feather
火 fire

Index of Characters and Phrases

Chineasy teaches mainly traditional Chinese (see p. 18). Where the traditional and simplified forms of a character are different, the traditional form is given first, followed by the simplified form. Where no distinction between forms is noted, the traditional and simplified forms of the character are the same.

Acknowledgments

This has been the hardest page to write in this book. I want to thank so many people, but I have only limited space. I am sometimes asked if I had any idea how successful Chineasy would be when I first created it. The truth is, I do not really understand what 'success' is. It is a Western concept that did not exist in my Taoist philosophy. However, if you were to ask me whether or not I believe that the creation of Chineasy is meaningful, then my answer would be a resounding 'yes'. It began as a personal project to encourage my British-born children to learn Chinese. I wanted to make language-teaching fun and easy, as well as effective. My TED Talk in California in 2013 made Chineasy available to the public for the first time. Since then, many people have helped to shape Chineasy. My team and I are constantly inspired by people from around the world sharing their stories, learning experiences and constructive advice. Parents and doctors have told us how their children or patients with learning difficulties started learning Chinese characters using Chineasy. When people express their appreciation, they do not realize that we, in fact, are the grateful ones, because their encouragement keeps us going.

The Chineasy characters have been drawn brilliantly by the amazing illustrator Noma Bar. I cannot count the number of nights, after I put my children to bed, that Noma and I were on the phone until the early hours, going through every character endless times. The later the hour, the wilder our ideas became. I hope our shared sense of humour shines through. Noma is a true artist, and it has been a great pleasure working with him.

I am very lucky to have a world-class team. For the past eight years, Dimple Nathwani has been making every aspect of my work and life function smoothly. She is a trusted friend and an ever-reliable colleague. Carissa Chan, a promising young trilingual graphic designer, has been with Chineasy since the very beginning; her contribution to the project is evident. Our research assistant, Rachel Liang, a qualified Chinese teacher, has helped us with our thirst for knowledge. This book would not have been possible without Noma, Dimple, Carissa and Rachel. I am grateful to them for putting up with me.

I also wish to thank the editor, Claire Chandler, and Lucas Dietrich, Adélia Sabatini and Rolf Grisebach of Thames & Hudson, who have been the driving force behind this book. I am grateful to our managers, Rafe Sagalyn and Liz Farrell of ICM and Karolina Sutton and Nicholas McDermott of Curtis Brown, for looking after us. I have appreciated discussions with and advice and support from Mark Sebba, Rohan Silva, David Kester, David Rowen, Valerie Wong, Joi Ito, Dana Bar, Deb Roy, Jayce Pei Yu Lee, Helen Cowley, G.J. Huang, Tom Wong (王文華), Yi-Ching Liao (廖怡景), Jackie Lin (林香君), Y.C. Chen (陳耀昌), Richard Davies, Huei-Tse Hou (侯惠澤), Fu-Sheng Qiu (邱復生), Zhicheng Lo (羅智成) and David Chuang (莊思凌). My sister Josephine Hsueh Tsao (薛筱瑩), a real Chinese teacher at the University of San Francisco, has been my role model since I was little.

My dearest and coolest friend, Judith Greenbury, continues to be my inspiration and greatest support. She is the one I call when I travel around the world. This book is to wish her a happy 92nd birthday.

My life is enriched by my dearest friends Suzy and Philip Rowley, Melissa and James Bethell, Myron Scholes, Erik Brynjolfsson, Ching-Chih Lu (盧敬植) and my sister Anchi Hsueh (薛安琪). They are part of my family and will always be. Ultimately, I hope I can continue connecting the dots between my beloved father (薛瑞芳) and mother (林峯子), daughter MuLan (慕嵐) and son MuAn (慕安).